Charting the Market

Mastering Technical Analysis for Savvy Trading

By

Nathan Venture, D

Charting the Market

Mastering Technical Analysis for Savvy Trading

Table of Contents

Introduction:
Embracing the Art of Technical
Analysis

Technical analysis is not just a tool; it's an art form that bridges the gap between the seemingly chaotic fluctuations of the market and a trader's quest for predictability and profitability. At its core, technical analysis involves studying past price movements and trading volumes to identify patterns and make informed predictions about future price movements. However, it's much more than just plotting lines on a chart. It's about understanding the psychology behind those patterns and leveraging that knowledge to make better trading decisions.

In today's fast-paced trading environment, the ability to swiftly interpret and act on market signals can be the difference between significant gains and catastrophic losses. With the proliferation of trading platforms and the increasing complexity of financial instruments, mastering the nuances of technical analysis has become more critical than ever. Whether you're a seasoned trader or a newcomer hoping to dip your toes into the trading world, the skills and insights gained from technical analysis offer invaluable support in making informed decisions.

Why is technical analysis essential? The financial markets are driven by supply and demand, emotions, economic indicators, and countless other factors. While fundamental analysis focuses on evaluating a company's financial health through its balance sheets and earnings reports, technical analysis zeroes in on historical price patterns, volumes, and trends. This provides traders an edge by allowing them to anticipate market movements rather than merely reacting to them.

One fundamental concept in technical analysis is the belief that history tends to repeat itself. Market participants exhibit consistent behaviors, and certain patterns become almost self-fulfilling prophecies. Recognizing these patterns gives traders a way to forecast potential price movements, identify entry and exit points, and manage their portfolio's risk effectively. The combination of such strategies empowers traders to navigate both bullish and bearish markets with confidence and agility.

Chart reading is a foundational skill for any technical analyst. Price charts condense immense amounts of information into a visual format that allows traders to quickly identify trends, reversals, and other critical market dynamics. Various chart types, including line charts, bar charts, and candlestick charts, each have their unique advantages and offer unique insights into market behavior. Mastering these tools is a stepping stone to deeper technical analysis concepts like trend identification and momentum trading.

Risk management stands as another pillar of effective trading. No matter how skilled a trader is in technical analysis, there will always be unpredictability in the markets. Integrating sound risk management strategies ensures that traders can withstand periods of market volatility and avoid the traps of emotional trading. Techniques such as setting stop-loss orders, diversified portfolio management, and position sizing are all part and parcel of a well-rounded trading plan.

A conversation about technical analysis wouldn't be complete without discussing the psychological aspect of trading. Emotions like fear and greed often drive market movements, and understanding these emotions can provide traders with an edge. Recognizing the signs of market sentiment and integrating them with technical indicators can often validate or call into question a potential market move. Behavioral finance, a key element of market psychology, indicates why traders act the way they do and how those actions influence market trends and patterns.

As we delve further into this book, you'll encounter a variety of technical indicators and tools that heighten your ability to read the markets accurately. From simple moving averages to sophisticated momentum oscillators, each tool offers a different lens through which to view market data. Knowing when and how to apply these indicators in real-world scenarios can significantly enhance your trading performance.

But knowledge alone isn't enough. The real magic happens when knowledge meets action. This book's ultimate aim is to arm you with the tools and confidence you need to take decisive, strategic actions in the markets. You'll learn how to build a rule-based trading system, backtest strategies, and keep a detailed trading journal. These practices help in evaluating performance and making necessary adjustments over time. The goal is to refine your trading tactics continually and adapt to ever-changing market conditions.

Moreover, it's crucial to remember that technical analysis is not an isolated discipline. Successful traders often integrate technical analysis with other forms of analysis and market knowledge for a more comprehensive approach. By combining technical signals with fundamental analysis and staying attuned to macroeconomic factors, traders can develop a holistic view of the market and further refine their decision-making processes.

So, whether you're an investor looking to sharpen your portfolio management skills, a day trader seeking to exploit short-term price movements, or a financial analyst aiming to offer more rounded advice, this book has something for you. As you navigate through the intricacies of technical analysis, you'll discover that this art form isn't just about numbers and charts. It's about mastering a disciplined, strategic approach to trading that balances risk and reward while continually evolving with the markets.

Let's embark on this journey together. By embracing the art of technical analysis, we'll equip ourselves with the knowledge, strategies, and mindset necessary to navigate the financial markets successfully. The road to becoming a proficient trader is paved with learning and practice. This book will act as your guide, illuminating the path ahead and providing the insights needed to achieve your trading aspirations.

Chapter 1:
The Foundation of Trading

To truly succeed in the world of trading, it's vital to build a robust foundation rooted in both knowledge and experience. This chapter serves as your cornerstone, setting the stage for all the strategies and techniques you'll explore later. We begin by understanding the complex landscape of the stock market, a dynamic ecosystem influenced by countless factors and ever-evolving trends. With this backdrop, we'll dive into market psychology, exploring the behavioral aspects that drive investor decision-making and market movements. By grasping these fundamental concepts, you'll develop the intuitive and analytical skills needed to navigate the markets effectively. Remember, a solid foundation isn't just about knowing how the market works— it's about mastering the mindset needed to thrive in this high-stakes arena.

Understanding the Stock Market Landscape

The stock market can be an intimidating and complex entity for traders and investors, whether you're a seasoned pro or a newbie. Grasping its foundational structure is critical for anyone looking to navigate its ups and downs successfully. The stock market isn't just about buying low and selling high; it's a complex network of exchanges, participants, regulations, and economic indicators. Every decision you make on this stage has rippling effects, and understanding these elements can empower you to make well-informed trading decisions.

At its core, the stock market serves as a platform for companies to raise capital by issuing shares to the public. These shares are then traded among investors. Stock exchanges, like the New York Stock Exchange (NYSE) and the NASDAQ, facilitate these transactions. Each exchange has its own set of rules, requirements, and listed companies, but all aim to provide a transparent and efficient marketplace. Familiarizing yourself with the major exchanges and their operating principles will give you a head start in understanding market dynamics.

Alongside exchanges, regulatory bodies play a crucial role in keeping the stock market fair and transparent. In the United States, the Securities and Exchange Commission (SEC) oversees securities transactions, ensuring that investors are protected against fraud and that markets operate efficiently. Regulatory news, changes in policies, or updates can profoundly impact market sentiment and, ultimately, stock prices. Staying informed about regulatory environments is essential for every trader.

Market participants range from individual retail investors to large institutional players like hedge funds, mutual funds, and pension funds. Each participant brings different strategies, objectives, and levels of resources to the table. Retail investors might focus on personal financial goals, while institutional investors often have larger sums of capital and a plethora of well-researched strategies. Institutional moves can considerably influence stock prices due to their significant buying power, making it wise for individual traders to keep an eye on these big players.

Another crucial aspect to grasp is the concept of market indices. Indices like the S&P 500, Dow Jones Industrial Average, and NASDAQ Composite represent the performance of a segment of the market. They serve as benchmarks for comparing individual stock performance. Understanding indices helps you gauge overall market conditions, identify trends, and make more educated trading choices. Whether you're trading individual stocks or engaging in index funds, knowing how indices function is invaluable.

Economic indicators also hold significant sway over market behaviors. Gross Domestic Product (GDP), employment figures, inflation rates, and interest rates are amongst the many factors that can impact market performance. For instance, lower interest rates often lead to higher stock prices as borrowing becomes cheaper, encouraging investment. Meanwhile, economic downturns revealed through sluggish GDP growth can lead to market declines. By staying updated with economic data releases, traders can better anticipate market movements.

It's vital to understand the concept of liquidity. Liquidity refers to how easily an asset can be bought or sold in the market without affecting its price. High liquidity means a more stable trading environment, while low liquidity can lead to high volatility and increased risk. Stocks from large-cap companies generally exhibit high liquidity, making them attractive for day trading and swing trading. Conversely, small-cap stocks may lack liquidity, though they can offer higher growth potential, balancing the risk-reward equation.

Corporate actions and events, such as earnings reports, dividends, stock splits, and mergers, can trigger significant price movements. Earnings reports typically reveal a company's financial health, providing traders with insights into future performance. Positive surprises might lead to stock price jumps, while disappointments can cause sharp declines. Keeping track of corporate calendars and understanding the implications of these events helps traders position themselves strategically.

Geopolitical events represent another layer of complexity. Trade wars, elections, and international conflicts can cause market instability. For example, tariffs on Chinese imports can affect American tech companies relying on Chinese manufacturing. Thus, a well-rounded trader stays aware of global events, as they often contribute to market volatility.

The advent of technology has also reshaped the stock market landscape. Algorithmic trading, high-frequency trading (HFT), and automated trading systems streamline processes, but also introduce new challenges and complexities. High-frequency traders use sophisticated algorithms to execute trades within milliseconds, capitalizing on minute price differences. While this adds liquidity and efficiency, it can also exacerbate market swings and pose challenges for individual traders. Understanding these technological advancements equips you to better interpret market activities and adversities.

Social sentiment and news also substantially impact stock prices. Media coverage, analyst reports, and social media buzz can all influence market perceptions and investor behavior. A positive article in a renowned financial magazine might cause a stock to soar, while a damaging tweet from a company's executive could send it plummeting. The rapid dissemination of information in the digital age requires traders to be alert and discerning in separating fact from noise.

A deeper look into behavioral finance reveals that human emotions and cognition can significantly affect market outcomes. Herd behavior, where individuals follow the collective actions of the market, can lead to bubbles and crashes. Recognizing these patterns helps traders avoid pitfalls and capitalize on opportunities. Remember, the stock market is not just a numbers game but also a psychological battle.

Lastly, a robust understanding of the stock market landscape requires one to stay educated continuously. Financial markets are dynamic and ever-evolving. Regulatory changes, technological innovations, and new economic paradigms continually shift the market's foundation. By cultivating a mindset of lifelong learning and staying updated with market developments, you won't just react to changes, but proactively adapt your strategies, enhancing your trading acumen.

Understanding the stock market landscape is about connecting the dots between exchanges, regulatory bodies, market participants, economic indicators, technology, corporate actions, geopolitical events, and psychology. This holistic perspective forms the bedrock of informed trading and investing, equipping you to timely identify opportunities and mitigate risks. Armed with this comprehensive knowledge, you'll be better positioned to master the nuanced art of stock market trading.

diving into market psychology

Understanding market psychology is pivotal for any trader aiming to navigate the complexities of the financial markets. At its core, market psychology involves interpreting the collective emotions, attitudes, and behaviors of market participants. Traders often rely on sentiment analysis to gauge market mood, recognizing that fear, greed, optimism, and uncertainty can drive price movements in ways that fundamentally disrupt traditional market theories. Mastering this psychological aspect arms traders with the insight to anticipate market shifts, identify contrarian opportunities, and mitigate the impact of irrational decisions. By delving into market psychology, traders can develop a more nuanced approach to decision-making, transforming potentially erratic markets into arenas of opportunity and strategic advantage.

Sentiment Analysis in Trading

Analysis is an indispensable tool in a trader's arsenal, particularly when dealing with the nuances of market psychology. At its core, sentiment analysis involves gauging the mood of the market participants. For traders, this means interpreting the collective feelings and attitudes toward a particular stock, sector, or the market as a whole, then leveraging that information for strategic decision-making. Sentiment can often drive market movements regardless of underlying fundamentals, making it crucial for traders to understand and interpret it effectively.

Understanding sentiment starts with recognizing its different forms: bullish, bearish, and neutral. Bullish sentiment indicates optimism, where traders expect prices to rise. Bearish sentiment, on the other hand, signifies pessimism, with expectations of falling prices. Neutral sentiment indicates uncertainty or indecision. Each of these sentiments can be measured through various means—news headlines, social media chatter, investor surveys, and options trading activity, to name a few.

One critical component of sentiment analysis is the analysis of news and media. News articles, press releases, and earnings reports can all dramatically shift market sentiment. Traders often use tools and platforms that aggregate and analyze news to determine whether the overall tone is positive, negative, or neutral. This process, often aided by natural language processing (NLP) techniques, helps traders extract actionable insights from vast amounts of textual data.

Social media has also emerged as a powerful sentiment indicator. Platforms like Twitter, Reddit, and StockTwits have become hotbeds of investor opinion and market speculation. By monitoring trends and discussions on these platforms, traders can garner real-time insight into market sentiment. Tools like sentiment analysis bots and algorithms can scan social media feeds for specific keywords and phrases, assessing the sentiment behind them to provide traders with as-it-happens updates.

The role of sentiment is particularly pronounced in short-term trading strategies, such as day trading and swing trading. Day traders may look to capitalize on short-term sentiment shifts caused by breaking news or social media trends. Swing traders, on the other hand, might use sentiment analysis to confirm or filter potential trading signals derived from technical indicators. By integrating sentiment insights into these strategies, traders can better time their entries and exits to align with prevailing market attitudes.

Sentiment indices and surveys, like the American Association of Individual Investors (AAII) Sentiment Survey or the Fear and Greed Index, offer another valuable perspective. These indices aggregate investor sentiment and present it in a quantifiable format, providing a snapshot of market emotions. When these indices reach extreme levels, they can act as contrarian indicators. For example, if the Fear and Greed Index shows extreme greed, that may signal an overheated market ripe for a pullback.

Another method for gauging sentiment involves examining options market data. The put-call ratio, which compares the volume of put options to call options, is a widely-used sentiment indicator. A high put-call ratio suggests bearish sentiment, while a low ratio indicates bullish sentiment. Additionally, the implied volatility of options can reveal the market's expectations of future volatility, impacting sentiment.

Implied volatility, often expressed through the Volatility Index (VIX), also provides essential sentiment insights. When the VIX is high, it indicates a heightened level of fear in the market, suggesting bearish sentiment. Conversely, a low VIX points to complacency or confidence, indicative of bullish sentiment. Monitoring these fluctuations can help traders anticipate potential market reversals or continuations.

Understanding sentiment analysis equips traders with a well-rounded perspective of market dynamics. Technical analysis provides objective data points, while sentiment analysis adds a subjective layer, accounting for the human emotions and psychological factors that drive market actions. By blending these two approaches, traders can develop a more robust trading strategy.

However, it's important to acknowledge the limitations of sentiment analysis. Sentiment can be fickle and subject to rapid change, making it challenging to rely on it exclusively. False signals and anomalies in sentiment data are not uncommon, necessitating careful interpretation and validation against other indicators. This is why a holistic approach, incorporating multiple forms of analysis, often yields the best results.

Moreover, sentiment analysis isn't just about gauging the mood of retail investors. Institutional sentiment also plays a crucial role. Large financial institutions and hedge funds have substantial market influence, and their sentiment can shape market movements significantly. Tools like the Commitment of Traders (COT) report, which details the positions of institutional traders, can provide invaluable insights into this aspect of sentiment.

For those looking to dive deeper into sentiment analysis, a variety of tools and platforms are available. Services like MarketPsych and StockTwits offer specialized sentiment analysis features tailored for traders. Additionally, many trading platforms now integrate sentiment indicators directly into their charting tools, making it easier than ever to incorporate sentiment analysis into your routine.

Sentiment Analysis in Trading isn't just a supplementary tool; it can also serve as a leading indicator. Unlike lagging indicators, which confirm past market movements, sentiment analysis can provide early signals about future price actions. When used effectively, it can help traders anticipate shifts in market momentum before they become evident in price action, offering a significant edge.

As you hone your trading skills, don't underestimate the power of understanding market sentiment. While not a standalone strategy, sentiment analysis can significantly enhance your trading toolkit. It gives you an additional layer of information, enriching your market perspective and making your trading decisions more informed and timely. Through diligent practice and ongoing learning, sentiment analysis can become an integral part of your trading success.

In conclusion, mastering sentiment analysis is a continuous journey. It requires staying updated with market news, monitoring social media trends, understanding various sentiment indicators, and interpreting institutional sentiment. However, the effort is worthwhile. By combining sentiment insights with technical analysis, you can cultivate a more comprehensive view of market dynamics. This holistic approach can ultimately empower you to navigate the financial markets with greater confidence and precision, setting you on a path toward consistent trading success.

Chapter 2:
Charting Your Course

Now that you've laid the groundwork for your trading journey, it's time to chart your course by mastering the art of reading price charts and selecting the right time frames to align with your trading style. Whether you're a day trader, swing trader, or a long-term investor, understanding the intricacies of price movements is essential. This chapter will guide you through interpreting charts beyond their basic elements, helping you discern critical patterns and trends that signal potential trading opportunities. By honing these skills, you'll gain a clearer vision of market dynamics, empowering you to make smarter, data-driven decisions. Confidence stems from clarity, and clarity begins with effectively charting your course in the complex landscape of financial markets.

Reading Price Charts: Beyond the Basics

Reading price charts is where the real magic happens in technical analysis. It's not just about recognizing patterns and setups. It's about understanding the language they speak. When you're looking at a price chart, you're essentially peering into the psychology of the market participants. Each bar, line, and candle tells a story—of fear, greed, hope, and despair. To navigate these waters effectively, we need to go beyond the basics and develop a nuanced understanding of price action.

At its core, a price chart is a graphical representation of an asset's historical price data. Sounds simple enough, right? But the complexity arises when you start interpreting the myriad of information it presents. A seasoned trader knows that it's not just about seeing the price, but comprehending the subtleties. For instance, the placement of price within a candlestick and its relation to prior candles can tell volumes about potential future movement.

Let's dive deeper into some essential yet often overlooked aspects of reading price charts. One key element is understanding the concept of "market structure." Market structure revolves around the ebb and flow of price movements. You might see higher highs and higher lows in an uptrend, or lower highs and lower lows in a downtrend. Recognizing these shifts is crucial because it helps identify trend reversals and continuations.

Imagine you're examining a chart and notice an ascending triangle forming—this is typically a bullish continuation pattern. Here, the highs keep meeting a resistance level, but the lows are progressively higher. This indicates that buyers are gaining confidence. On the flip side, a descending triangle might signal bearish continuation. These nuanced patterns can offer significant trading opportunities if you know how to spot them.

Volume is another critical factor to consider when reading price charts. Volume confirms the strength of a price move. If a stock breaks out of a key resistance level on high volume, it's more likely to sustain the move compared to a breakout on low volume. Think of volume as the fuel that propels price movement. Charts with accompanying volume bars can help distinguish genuine moves from false breakouts.

Don't forget about the power of multiple time frame analysis. Viewing the same asset across different time frames can offer a comprehensive picture. For example, a trend that looks solid on a daily chart might show signs of weakness on a shorter time frame, such as a

15-minute or hourly chart. Combining these perspectives allows traders to make well-informed decisions, understanding both the macro and micro views of market activity.

Then there's the matter of identifying support and resistance levels. These levels are psychological barriers where the price tends to stall and reverse. Support levels indicate where buying interest is strong enough to overcome selling pressure, while resistance levels indicate where selling interest is robust enough to overcome buying pressure. Recognizing these levels can aid in placing effective stops and targets, enhancing risk management.

Advanced technical traders often use moving averages to filter out the noise of daily price fluctuations. Simple Moving Averages (SMA) and Exponential Moving Averages (EMA) smooth out price data and help identify the underlying trend. For instance, the 50-day and 200-day moving averages are commonly watched by traders and can serve as significant support or resistance levels themselves.

Moreover, the interplay between different technical indicators can provide a richer context. For instance, combining Relative Strength Index (RSI) with Moving Average Convergence Divergence (MACD) can offer deeper insights. If RSI shows an asset is overbought while MACD starts to signal a bearish crossover, it might be time to prepare for a price correction.

Chart patterns, too, play their part, but to understand them fully, one must delve into the psychology behind them. Patterns like Head and Shoulders, Double Tops and Bottoms, and Cup and Handle each tell a story of market sentiment. A Head and Shoulders pattern, for example, often indicates a shift from bullish to bearish sentiment. Recognizing these patterns early can offer a tactical advantage.

The use of Fibonacci retracement levels adds another layer of sophistication. Traders use Fibonacci levels to identify potential support and resistance areas created by the natural ebb and flow of market cycles. The key Fibonacci levels—highlighting 38.2%, 50%, and 61.8% retracements—often align with significant price reactions. Incorporating these levels into your analysis can fine-tune entry and exit points in your trades.

Lastly, it's essential to stay tuned to the broader market context. No chart exists in a vacuum. Economic indicators, geopolitical events, and market sentiment all impact price action. By combining technical analysis with an understanding of these broader factors, traders can navigate the market with more confidence and precision.

Reading price charts is akin to learning a language. The more fluent you become, the better you'll be at interpreting what the market is communicating. It's a blend of art and science, requiring a mix of analytical rigor and intuitive understanding. As you hone these skills, remember that continuous learning and practice are your best allies. The market will always have lessons to teach, and the price chart is its blackboard. Embrace it, and let it guide your trading journey.

Time Frames and Trading Styles

Every trader knows that choosing the right time frame and trading style is crucial for success. Whether you're day trading to capitalize on short-term price movements or investing for the long haul, the time frame you select will significantly impact your strategy and outcomes. For day traders, who thrive on intra-day volatility, minute-by-minute charts are essential. Swing traders, on the other hand, benefit from daily or weekly charts to capture significant price moves over days or weeks. Long-term investors look at monthly and yearly charts, focusing on macro trends and fundamental shifts. Understanding the nuances of these time frames and aligning them with your trading style can sharpen your decision-making, optimize risk management, and ultimately enhance your investment journey.

Day Trading vs. Swing Trading vs. Long-Term Investing

These strategies encompass a critical examination of three distinct trading styles, each presenting its own set of opportunities, challenges, and strategies. Understanding these differences is vital for any trader or investor aiming to maximize returns while managing risk effectively. First, let's dive into day trading, a fast-paced style that requires swift decision-making and a keen eye for market movements.

Day trading involves buying and selling securities within the same trading day, sometimes even within minutes or seconds. The goal is to capitalize on small price fluctuations, which can be realized through high volume and leverage. Traders utilize various technical indicators, such as moving averages, RSI, and MACD, to make informed decisions. This trading style demands a comprehensive understanding of market charts and trends and a disciplined approach to risk management. Quick exits are essential to lock in profits or cut losses, and emotional discipline can't be overstated.

Emotional discipline in day trading can be the difference between success and failure. Professional day traders often have predefined entry and exit points and adhere to their trading plan without letting fear or greed influence their decisions. The need for constant attention to the market means this trading style can be highly stressful and time-consuming. It's not uncommon for day traders to use high-frequency trading algorithms and other technological tools to gain a competitive edge.

Swing trading, on the other hand, typically involves holding positions for several days to a few weeks. The objective is to capture short- to medium-term gains in a stock over a few days to weeks. Swing traders rely heavily on technical analysis but also consider fundamental analysis to some extent. They aim to identify and exploit market 'swings,' hence the name, which can occur in both trending and volatile markets.

Swing trading is often considered more accessible for part-time traders who cannot commit to the full-time focus required for day trading. This style allows for more flexibility since the trades span several days or weeks, giving traders time to make informed decisions without the constant pressure of real-time market fluctuations. While it still requires a solid understanding of technical indicators and chart patterns, swing trading generally involves fewer transactions than day trading, which can reduce transaction costs.

The risk management strategies in swing trading also differ from day trading. Swing traders use stop-loss orders to protect against substantial losses and may also use position sizing to manage risk. The use of set entry and exit points, based on technical indicators like support and resistance levels, helps mitigate emotional decision-making. This trading style is ideal for those looking to take advantage of price movements without the frenetic pace of day trading.

Long-term investing is a fundamentally different approach compared to day trading and swing trading. This strategy focuses on buying and holding securities for extended periods, often years or even decades. The objective is to benefit from the company's growth over time and compound returns. Investors in this category often look at fundamental indicators such as earnings reports, dividends, and broader economic conditions rather than short-term technical signals.

Long-term investing is rooted in the belief that markets tend to rise over the long run, despite short-term volatility. This approach allows investors to ride out market downturns without panic selling. It involves a rigorous analysis of company fundamentals, including financial health, sector performance, and competitive advantages. Long-term investors also benefit from minimized transaction costs and the power of compounding returns over time.

In contrast to the emotionally intensive day trading and moderately paced swing trading, long-term investing takes a more laid-back approach. The focus is on building a diversified portfolio that can weather market fluctuations and provide steady returns. Key metrics such as price-to-earnings ratios, dividend yields, and revenue growth are often scrutinized. This method also aligns well with strategies like dollar-cost averaging, which helps in mitigating the impact of market volatility by spreading out investments over time.

Balancing Risk and Reward in these trading styles is crucial. The high-frequency nature of day trading offers the potential for significant rewards but comes with equally high risks. The fast-paced environment leaves little room for error, making robust risk management strategies, such as tight stop-loss orders, essential. Swing trading, while less intense, still requires diligent monitoring and responsive actions to capture profits. Long-term investing offers a more relaxed approach, relying heavily on thorough research and patience to achieve success over time.

Understanding your personality and risk tolerance is the key to choosing the right trading style. If you're someone who thrives under pressure and can make quick decisions, day trading might suit you. If you prefer a balance between active trading and the opportunity to analyze and act deliberately, swing trading could be a better fit. Lastly, if you are patient and prefer to let your investments grow over time with less frequent buying and selling, long-term investing might be the best option.

In conclusion, **Day Trading vs. Swing Trading vs. Long-Term Investing** requires a thorough understanding of different trading strategies, risk management, and individual temperament. Each style has its set of advantages and challenges, and the key to success lies in choosing the one that best aligns with your overall trading philosophy and goals. Continually educating yourself and staying disciplined are imperative, regardless of the trading style you choose.

Chapter 3:
The Power of Trend Analysis

In the dynamic world of trading, harnessing the power of trend analysis can make all the difference between success and missed opportunities. Recognizing and riding trends allow traders to capitalize on market momentum, turning insights into profitable actions. It's about understanding the ebbs and flows of price movements and deciphering patterns that reveal the market's underlying intentions. Trend analysis isn't just about spotting short-term gains—it's about grasping broader market movements that can inform smarter investment strategies and risk management. This vital skill empowers traders to identify when to enter and exit positions, maximizing returns while minimizing potential losses. Combining trend analysis with key concepts like support and resistance gives traders a comprehensive toolset to navigate the complex market landscape with confidence and precision.

Identifying Trends and Their Significance

Understanding the trends in the market is akin to deciphering a complex, evolving narrative. Trends form the backbone of technical analysis, offering traders and investors a way to navigate the often turbulent and unpredictable financial markets. Recognizing these patterns isn't just about identifying movements; it's about interpreting the deeper market sentiment and future possibilities they reveal. Whether it's a bullish or bearish trend, knowing how to spot and analyze these trends can be the difference between success and failure in trading.

Being proficient in trend identification allows traders to make informed decisions based on price movements over periods. At its core, a trend is the general direction in which a market or the price of an asset is moving. There are three primary types of trends: uptrend (bullish), downtrend (bearish), and sideways trend (consolidation). Each of these trends holds significant implications for trading strategies and risk management.

An uptrend is characterized by higher highs and higher lows, signaling that the market's sentiment is predominantly positive, with buyers driving prices upward. Traders look to capitalize on this optimism by buying into the market and riding the wave of increasing prices. Key indicators of an uptrend include moving averages trending upwards and confirming higher peaks in price action.

Conversely, a downtrend is distinguished by lower highs and lower lows, indicating a bearish market sentiment where sellers outnumber buyers, pushing prices lower. Traders may look to profit through short-selling strategies or by exiting long positions to minimize losses. Confirmatory signals, such as decreasing moving averages and declining price peaks, often validate a downtrend.

Sideways trends, where prices move within a narrow range without showing a clear upward or downward trajectory, often signal market indecision. During these times, traders might refrain from taking significant positions, as the potential for false signals is higher. Recognizing a sideways trend can help in preserving capital and waiting for more definitive trends to emerge.

Identifying these trends requires the use of various technical tools and indicators. Trendlines, for instance, are graphical representations that highlight the direction and strength of a trend. Drawing an upward trendline involves connecting successive higher lows, while a downward trendline connects lower highs. These lines provide visual cues that help traders understand trend dynamics and potential trend reversals.

Moreover, understanding the significance of trends entails recognizing when they might change. Trend reversals occur when an uptrend transitions to a downtrend, or vice versa. Certain chart patterns and technical indicators, such as the Moving Average Convergence Divergence (MACD) or Relative Strength Index (RSI), can signal when a trend change is imminent. Spotting these reversal signs early on can provide lucrative entry points or timely exit strategies.

Consider the importance of time frames in trend analysis. Trends can vary drastically across different time frames — what appears as a robust uptrend on a daily chart might look like a brief rally in the context of a weekly chart. Day traders may focus on minute-by-minute trends, while long-term investors might rely on monthly or yearly trends. The choice of time frame depends on individual trading styles and objectives, adding another layer of nuance to trend identification.

Seasoned traders often employ moving averages to smooth out price data and better identify trends. Simple Moving Averages (SMAs) and Exponential Moving Averages (EMAs) serve as dynamic support and resistance levels. When a shorter-term moving average crosses above a longer-term one, it signals a potential uptrend. Conversely, a bearish signal is generated when a shorter-term moving average crosses below a longer-term one.

Furthermore, understanding support and resistance levels is fundamental to trend analysis. Support levels are price points where a downtrend can pause due to a concentration of buying interest. Resistance levels, on the other hand, are price points where an uptrend can stall, as selling interests outweigh buying interests. Identifying these levels on a price chart aids in predicting potential breakout or breakdown points and trend continuation or reversal.

The role of volume in confirming trends cannot be understated. Volume analysis, which involves assessing the number of shares or contracts traded in a security or market, offers insights into the strength of a trend. An uptrend accompanied by high volume suggests strong buying interest, while a downtrend with rising volume indicates robust selling pressure. Volume spikes at key resistance or support levels can also validate breakouts or breakdowns, providing actionable trading opportunities.

Combining multiple indicators and techniques enhances the reliability of trend analysis. For instance, using a combination of moving averages, trendlines, and volume can offer a more holistic view of market conditions. Employing a convergence of indicators helps filter out noise and reduces the likelihood of false signals, leading to more accurate trend identification.

Traders should also appreciate the psychological aspects embedded within trends. Human behavior and market psychology often drive trends. Bull markets can create a self-fulfilling cycle of optimism, where high prices attract more buyers, propelling prices further up. Bear markets, conversely, can breed pessimism, causing panic selling and further declines. Recognizing these psychological underpinnings enables traders to position themselves advantageously in line with market sentiment.

Finally, it's essential to keep in mind that no trend lasts forever. Markets are cyclical, and trends can shift due to various factors, including economic data releases, geopolitical events, and changes in investor sentiment. Staying vigilant and flexible in your approach ensures that you're not caught off guard by sudden market shifts. Utilizing a disciplined trading plan with clear entry and exit criteria helps manage the risks associated with trend reversals.

In summary, identifying trends and understanding their significance is a pivotal skill in the arsenal of any trader or investor. It requires a blend of technical expertise, psychological acumen, and strategic flexibility. By mastering trend analysis, traders can better anticipate market movements, optimize their trading strategies, and ultimately achieve greater success in their financial endeavors.

Support and Resistance: Key Concepts for Traders

When diving into the realm of trend analysis, understanding support and resistance is absolutely crucial for any trader. These key concepts help identify points where prices tend to pause or reverse, acting as psychological markers driven by market sentiment. Support levels signify where demand is strong enough to halt a downtrend, while resistance levels indicate where selling pressure is sufficient to cap an uptrend. By mastering these concepts, traders can make more informed decisions, pinpoint optimal entry and exit points, and effectively manage risks. The art of recognizing these levels empowers traders to anticipate market movements, leveraging historical data and price patterns to their strategic advantage.

Trendlines and Channels

Trendlines and Channels are instrumental tools in the technical analyst's toolkit, offering a clear visual representation of price direction and potential future movement. At their core, trendlines are simple— they connect successive lows in an uptrend or successive highs in a downtrend. This simplicity, however, belies their power. Trendlines can act as dynamic support and resistance levels, providing traders with actionable insights about the market's inherent structure.

Drawing a trendline correctly is essential. In an uptrend, you connect the valleys (or lows), while in a downtrend, you connect the peaks (or highs). The more points a trendline touches, the more validated it becomes, making its break significant. When price action respects a trendline, it signals the strength of the current trend. Conversely, a break indicates a potential shift in market sentiment, triggering potential trade opportunities.

The secret to leveraging trendlines effectively lies in their application across various time frames. Intraday traders may look at 15-minute charts to capture short-term price movements, while swing traders might examine daily or weekly charts for broader trends. This multi-time frame analysis ensures that you aren't blindsided by larger trends overshadowing your strategy. Mixing different time frames can also offer confirmation; for instance, an intraday trendline break aligned with a daily trendline can be a strong signal.

Channels take the concept of trendlines a step further. By drawing parallel lines above and below a primary trendline, channels encapsulate the price action of a security within two boundaries. These upper and lower bounds create a "channel" through which price fluctuates. Traders use channels to identify potential reversal points, aiming to buy at the lower boundary (support) and sell at the upper boundary (resistance). A well-defined channel not only highlights the prevailing trend but also provides well-defined risk parameters.

There are primarily three types of channels: ascending, descending, and horizontal. Ascending channels, also known as rising channels, are characterized by higher highs and higher lows, indicating an uptrend. Traders who recognize an ascending channel may consider buying near the channel's support line and selling near the resistance. On the other hand, descending channels, or falling channels, show lower highs and lower lows, signaling a downtrend. In this case, short-selling at the resistance and covering positions near the support can be a profitable strategy.

Horizontal channels, or sideways channels, indicate a range-bound market where prices oscillate between parallel support and resistance levels with no clear trend direction. In such scenarios, swing traders often capitalize on frequent reversals within the channel. Recognizing the type of channel your market is in can significantly sharpen your trading edge, providing clarity and confidence in your trading decisions.

Drawing channels requires precision and practice. Start by plotting a trendline that connects either the highs or lows of the price action. Then, create a parallel line that captures the highs for an ascending channel or the lows for a descending channel. The distance between these lines should accommodate most price fluctuations within the trend, though occasional spikes may breach the channel boundaries. Patience is key here; your first draft of a channel might need several adjustments as new price data comes in.

Trading strategies involving trendlines and channels aren't just about identifying these formations but also understanding market behavior around them. Trendline bounces and channel boundaries often coincide with increased volume, signaling strong interest at these levels. Watch for volume spikes as they can confirm the validity of a trendline or channel support/resistance, giving you more confidence in your trade setup. Additionally, combining trendlines and channels with other technical indicators, such as moving averages or stochastic oscillators, can further validate your analysis and enhance your strategies.

Beyond just application, recognizing the psychological underpinning associated with these patterns is crucial. Trendlines and channels visually represent market consensus and collective psychology, showing you where buyers and sellers are willing to engage. When prices consistently bounce off a trendline, it indicates unwavering trader behavior anchored in that pattern. Conversely, a break of a trendline or channel signals a shift in trader psychology, often triggering stops and new positions, leading to a surge in volatility and momentum.

It's also essential to recognize that markets do not move in straight lines. They ebb and flow, influenced by a multitude of factors from economic data releases to geopolitical events. Hence, it's not uncommon for price to overshoot trendlines and channels. The key is distinguishing between a genuine trend reversal and a temporary overshoot. Paying attention to closing prices rather than intraday spikes can provide more reliable signals.

Let's not forget the adaptability of trendlines and channels. They are not static; as market conditions evolve, so should your trendlines and channels. Redrawing them to reflect the most recent price action is crucial for keeping your analysis relevant. Adapting to changing market dynamics ensures that your technical analysis remains an accurate and powerful tool in your trading arsenal.

It's worthwhile to incorporate channels into your broader trading plan, acting as a framework for understanding price fluctuations. Whether you're swing trading, day trading, or investing for the long term, having clearly defined trendlines and channels offers a roadmap to navigate the chaotic and often unpredictable nature of the markets. These structures serve as signposts, guiding you to make more rational and disciplined trading decisions.

Remember, mastering trendlines and channels requires both study and practice. It's one thing to read about them and another to consistently apply them in live trading. Start by backtesting various securities to see how trendlines and channels behaved historically. Use demo accounts to practice drawing and trading them without risking capital. Over time, as your skill improves, the application of these tools will become second nature, and you'll find yourself identifying profitable opportunities with greater ease and confidence.

Trendlines and channels are not just about identifying areas of interest; they are about understanding the construction of market trends and patterns. They're about seeing where the market has been and anticipating where it's likely to go. Integrating these tools into your analysis is like learning a new language—the language of price action. With dedication and consistent application, you'll harness the full potential of trendlines and channels, turning market movements into profitable trading opportunities.

Chapter 4:
Volume and Volatility

As we transition from trend analysis to the intricate landscape of volume and volatility, it's pivotal to grasp how these elements serve as the market's bloodstream and heartbeat. Volume, essentially the count of shares or contracts traded, acts as a barometer for market activity, offering insights into the strength of a price movement. High volume confirms trends, while low volume may suggest a lack of conviction. Volatility, on the other hand, is a dual-edged sword, representing the rate at which prices increase or decrease for a given set of returns, often swinging between euphoric highs and panic-laden lows. This dynamic nature can be measured using indicators like the VIX, commonly referred to as the "fear gauge." Balancing these forces, proficient traders not only harness volume to validate their positions but also embrace volatility to spot lucrative opportunities and manage risk effectively. In doing so, they navigate the often choppy waters of the financial markets with a sense of precision and confidence that's born from understanding these foundational elements.

Volume: The Fuel of the Markets

In the bustling world of trading, volume serves as the lifeblood that fuels market movements. Understanding volume, and the signals it provides, is essential for any trader looking to make informed decisions. Volume represents the total number of shares or contracts traded for a security during a given period. High volume often correlates with significant market events or shifts, providing clear insight into market sentiment. Essentially, it measures the intensity of trading activity, which, in turn, reflects the strength of a price movement.

Volume is more than just a count of trades; it signifies the conviction behind price moves. When prices rise or fall, the volume can help determine whether the trend is robust or weak. For instance, if a stock's price increases on high volume, it indicates strong buyer interest, suggesting that the price may continue to rise. Conversely, a price move on low volume could be misleading and possibly short-lived.

Consider volume as the exclamation mark in the sentence of market activity. It emphasizes and confirms what's happening in the market. For example, a breakout from a resistance level accompanied by a significant increase in volume suggests that the breakout is genuine and likely to sustain. This is because the high volume shows widespread interest and participation from traders.

The relationship between volume and price movement also extends to trend reversals. A sudden spike in volume often precedes a reversal. This is because heightened volume represents a struggle between buyers and sellers, and a subsequent change in direction suggests that the prevailing trend may be exhausted. Observing volume can alert traders to potential reversals, allowing them to adjust their strategies accordingly.

It's crucial to understand the volume-price relationship to make better trading decisions. For instance, during a downtrend, decreasing volume may indicate that sellers are losing interest, potentially signaling a forthcoming bounce or reversal. Similarly, during an uptrend, if volume starts to dwindle, the rally may be running out of steam.

One of the key tools traders use to analyze volume is the Volume Moving Average (VMA). It's similar to price moving averages but applied to volume. By smoothing out short-term fluctuations, VMAs help traders see the bigger picture of volume trends. A rising VMA alongside rising prices suggests healthy buying interest, while a declining VMA with rising prices may warn of potential weakness.

Traders also often use volume indicators like the On-Balance Volume (OBV), which adds volume on up days and subtracts it on down days. This cumulative volume line helps traders identify whether volume is flowing into or out of a security. Positive OBV trends indicate accumulation, while negative trends suggest distribution. This can be especially useful in confirming price movements and anticipating price direction.

In addition to individual stock volume, market-wide volume can offer important clues. For instance, spikes in overall market volume often coincide with major news events or economic data releases, reflecting heightened investor interest and uncertainty. By paying attention to these volume spikes, traders can stay ahead of potential market volatility.

Understanding the role of volume in trading isn't just about interpreting data; it's about crafting a narrative of market activity. Each spike and lull in volume tells a story about market behavior and trader psychology. This narrative helps traders make strategic decisions, from entering positions to knowing when to hold or exit.

Volume analysis also plays a crucial role in identifying and validating technical patterns. Whether it's a head and shoulders, double top, or triangle, volume patterns often provide the final piece of confirmation. For instance, in a head and shoulders pattern, increasing volume on the left shoulder and declining volume on the head suggests weakening buyer interest, and a subsequent increase on the right shoulder confirms seller dominance.

Furthermore, trading volume can indicate market liquidity, which is critical for executing large trades without significantly impacting the market price. High volume means higher liquidity, allowing traders to enter or exit positions more smoothly. Low volume, on the other hand, can lead to price slippage and increased transaction costs.

Seasonal and cyclical factors also influence volume. Some periods, like year-end or quarterly earnings seasons, naturally see higher volumes due to increased trading activity, as investors reposition their portfolios. Understanding these patterns helps traders anticipate and adapt to changing market conditions.

Advanced traders often integrate volume analysis into their algorithmic trading strategies. By incorporating volume metrics into their models, they can develop more robust and predictive trading systems. For instance, algorithms can adjust their trading frequency or position sizes based on real-time volume data, enhancing their adaptability and precision.

Finally, volume serves as a bridge between technical analysis and fundamental analysis. While technical analysis focuses on price patterns and indicators, fundamental analysis looks at a company's financial health and macroeconomic factors. Volume, with its ability to reflect market sentiment, helps validate and complement both areas of analysis, offering a holistic view of the market.

In summary, volume is the pulse of the market, providing essential insights into market dynamics and trader sentiment. By mastering volume analysis, traders can enhance their decision-making, manage risks more effectively, and ultimately achieve better trading outcomes. Embrace the power of volume, and let it guide you toward more informed and confident trading strategies.

Volatility: Friend or Foe?

Volatility often feels like a double-edged sword, presenting both opportunities and threats for traders and investors alike. When market movements are pronounced, savvy traders can exploit these fluctuations to capture significant gains. At the same time, heightened volatility can be a harbinger of increased risk, requiring careful risk management strategies to prevent substantial losses. Embracing volatility necessitates an understanding of its causes and characteristics, empowering you to make calculated decisions rather than being driven by fear or greed. It's all about leveraging the right tools, and when used effectively, volatility can indeed become a powerful ally in your trading arsenal.

Understanding the VIX

The Volatility Index, more commonly known as the VIX, serves as a powerful tool for traders and investors alike. Dubbed the "fear gauge" of the market, the VIX offers a quantifiable measure of market risk and investors' sentiment. Developed by the Chicago Board Options Exchange (CBOE) in 1993, the VIX calculates a 30-day forward-looking volatility derived from S&P 500 index option prices. In simpler terms, it reflects expectations of stock market volatility over the next month. The technical nuances of the VIX make it indispensable for both risk management and tactical trading.

Traders use the VIX to gauge market anxiety; higher values suggest increased market turbulence, while lower values imply market stability. A VIX reading above 30 often indicates high volatility associated with investor fear or uncertainty, while levels below 20 suggest complacency and relative calm. However, interpreting the VIX isn't always straightforward. While a high VIX signals caution, it can also present lucrative trading opportunities for those who thrive in volatile environments.

Why does the VIX matter so much? Volatility often precedes major market moves. High VIX levels usually accompany sharp market declines, but they can also signal the bottom of a bearish trend, providing a potential entry point for opportunistic traders. The VIX's responsiveness to macroeconomic events, corporate earnings, geopolitical tensions, and even natural disasters makes it a dynamic and timely indicator.

A deeper dive into the VIX reveals its construction. At its core, the index calculates the weighted average of the implied volatilities for a range of options with different strike prices. Specifically, it looks at the first and second-month out-of-the-money S&P 500 puts and calls, a method that captures the market's forward-looking sentiment. By focusing on a range of strike prices, the VIX provides a comprehensive snapshot of market expectations.

The VIX doesn't just move on its own; it's deeply intertwined with investor psychology. Human behavior tends to oscillate between fear and greed, and the VIX captures these emotional swings in real-time. High volatility often results from panic selling, while low volatility can signify investor complacency or overconfidence. By monitoring VIX levels, traders can gain insight into crowd behavior and anticipate shifts in market trends.

Another strategic use of the VIX is in options trading. Options traders often use the VIX to price their contracts, influencing their strategies on whether to buy or sell puts and calls. When the VIX is low, the cost of options decreases, which may entice traders to buy options as a hedge against potential market shifts. Conversely, during periods of high VIX, the elevated cost of options might sway traders to sell premium.

The VIX isn't just limited to the world of equity markets; its principles apply broadly across different asset classes. For instance, bonds, commodities, and currencies also exhibit their own forms of volatility. While these markets may not have a direct equivalent to the VIX, the underlying concept of measuring and interpreting volatility remains the same.

Furthermore, the VIX serves as a critical component in portfolio risk management. Investors use the VIX to assess the vulnerability of their portfolios to market shocks. A rising VIX could prompt actions such as increasing cash holdings, diversifying investments, or employing hedging strategies. Essentially, understanding the VIX allows investors to be proactive rather than reactive, fostering a more resilient investment approach.

The VIX, however, is not without its limitations. Being a forward-looking indicator, it is based on market expectations rather than concrete events. Therefore, it is susceptible to rapid shifts in sentiment and may sometimes produce misleading signals. For instance, temporary spikes in the VIX might result from short-term news events that do not have a lasting impact on market fundamentals.

Nevertheless, the VIX's predictive power is generally respected in the trading community. Historical data shows that sharp increases in VIX levels frequently coincide with market corrections or bear markets. Conversely, sustained low VIX levels often precede periods of gradual market appreciation. However, traders must be cautious not to rely solely on the VIX, as it should complement other technical and fundamental analysis tools.

Many traders incorporate the VIX into broader trading systems. One common strategy is the "VIX and S&P 500" approach, where traders use VIX readings in conjunction with S&P 500 chart patterns to time their trades. For example, a simultaneous spike in the VIX and a breakdown in S&P 500 support levels could signal a strong selling opportunity. Conversely, a plummeting VIX paired with a bullish reversal pattern in the S&P 500 might indicate a lucrative buying moment.

In recent years, the proliferation of VIX derivatives has added another dimension to trading. Financial instruments such as VIX futures, options, and exchange-traded products (ETPs) enable traders to speculate directly on the VIX itself. These products offer the potential for significant gains, but also come with heightened risks and complexities, necessitating a sophisticated understanding of both the VIX and the instruments being traded.

To sum up, the VIX is indispensable for anyone seriously engaged in the markets. Its ability to provide insight into market sentiment and future volatility means it should be a staple in any trader's toolkit. Whether you are a day trader seeking short-term opportunities or a long-term investor managing risk, understanding the VIX can significantly enhance your market strategies. In the fast-paced world of trading, where every edge counts, the VIX offers a crucial vantage point from which to gauge potential market moves and align your actions accordingly.

Chapter 5:
Mastering Moving Averages

M oving averages are pivotal tools in a trader's arsenal, serving as both a lens to smooth out market noise and a compass to guide trading decisions. By averaging price data over specific time periods, moving averages create a dynamic line that evolves with market conditions, highlighting trends and potential reversals. Simple Moving Averages (SMAs) offers clarity by giving equal weight to all data points, whereas Exponential Moving Averages (EMAs) give greater importance to recent prices, enhancing their responsiveness. Mastering the balance between SMAs and EMAs allows traders to refine their timing and improve their decision-making process. Observing the interplay of moving averages, particularly crossovers, can generate powerful buy or sell signals, marking precise entry and exit points. As you delve deeper into the nuances of moving averages, their strategic application will empower you to navigate the markets with greater precision and confidence, setting the stage for achieving your trading goals.

Simple and Exponential Moving Averages

Moving averages are a cornerstone in the toolkit of any serious trader or investor. Whether you're analyzing short-term price fluctuations or long-term market trends, understanding moving averages can significantly enhance your decision-making process. They offer a smoothed perspective on the chaotic nature of price movements and can be adapted to suit various trading styles and objectives.

Simple Moving Averages (SMA) are the most straightforward type of moving average. They calculate the average price of a security over a specific number of periods. For instance, a 10-day SMA adds the closing prices for the past 10 days and divides that total by 10. This average is then plotted on a chart to create a smoothed line that eliminates most of the 'noise' created by daily price fluctuations.

The strength of the SMA lies in its simplicity. It helps traders quickly spot the overall direction of the market. If the SMA is sloping upwards, it generally signifies an uptrend, while a downward sloping SMA indicates a downtrend. However, the SMA has its limitations. It responds slowly to sudden price changes, making it less effective in fast-moving markets.

On the other hand, Exponential Moving Averages (EMA) give more weight to recent prices, making them more responsive to new information. This attribute makes EMAs particularly useful for shorter-term trading strategies where quick reactions to price changes are crucial. For instance, in a 10-day EMA, the most recent prices will have a more significant impact on the average, making it quicker to signal trend changes compared to the SMA.

While both SMA and EMA are designed to smooth out price data, they each offer unique advantages and should be chosen based on your trading needs. If your focus is on long-term trends, the slower, more stately action of the SMA might be preferable. If you need to act on short-term signals, the faster responsiveness of the EMA could be more beneficial.

One common application of moving averages is to generate entry and exit signals. For instance, when a short-term SMA crosses above a long-term SMA, it's often viewed as a bullish sign, signaling a potential buy. Conversely, when a short-term SMA crosses below a long-term SMA, it could indicate a bearish signal, advising a potential sell. This concept, known as a crossover, is a fundamental technique used by traders to time their trades.

It's essential to recognize that the choice of periods for your moving averages can significantly impact the signals you receive. Shorter periods can offer more timely signals but tend to come with more false alarms. Longer periods provide more reliable signals but with delays. Striking a balance between reliability and timeliness is key in selecting the right moving averages for your trading strategy.

Besides using moving averages for trend identification and entry/exit signals, they can also serve as dynamic support and resistance levels. Prices often retrace back to their moving averages during trending markets, offering potential entry points in the direction of the prevailing trend. For example, in a strong uptrend, the price might repeatedly bounce off the 50-day EMA, providing traders opportunities to add to their positions.

Similarly, moving averages can act as stop-loss triggers. Placing your stop-loss orders just below a key moving average can protect your position if the overall trend reverses. This method provides a logical and flexible approach to risk management, adjusting naturally with the price movements of the market.

Combining different types and periods of moving averages can create a more nuanced view of the market. For instance, employing a shorter-period EMA alongside a longer-period SMA can help you capture both short-term volatility and long-term trends. This dual approach can enhance your ability to anticipate market movements and better time your trades.

It's also beneficial to combine moving averages with other technical indicators. For instance, incorporating momentum oscillators, such as the Relative Strength Index (RSI) or the Moving Average Convergence Divergence (MACD), can provide additional context to the signals generated by your moving averages. This multi-faceted approach can greatly improve the accuracy of your trading signals.

Learning to master moving averages isn't just about understanding how they work; it's about integrating them into a broader strategy that aligns with your trading goals. Moving averages are versatile tools, but their effectiveness hinges on how well they're tailored to your specific trading style and market conditions.

In essence, moving averages offer guidance amidst market turbulence, smoothing out volatility and illuminating the underlying trends. They're not infallible but, when used correctly, they can provide a significant edge. Like any tool in trading, constant practice, back-testing, and adjustments are necessary to hone your strategy and make moving averages work for you.

Your journey into mastering moving averages starts with comprehending their fundamental principles and evolves with continuous learning and adaptation. As you weave these powerful tools into your trading repertoire, you'll find that they not only simplify the complex world of market movements but also empower you to make more calculated and confident trading decisions.

Crossovers and Signals: Timing Your Trade

Timing is everything in trading, and understanding moving average crossovers can be a powerful weapon in your toolkit. One of the most straightforward yet effective ways to identify potential buy and sell signals is through moving average crossovers. These occur when a shorter-term moving average crosses above or below a longer-term moving average. While the concept is simple, its implications are profound, giving traders a clear visual cue on when to enter or exit the market.

Let's begin with the golden cross and the death cross, terms that many market enthusiasts swear by. A golden cross happens when a short-term moving average, typically the 50-day moving average, crosses above a long-term moving average like the 200-day moving average. This is often seen as a bullish sign, suggesting that upward momentum is building. Conversely, a death cross occurs when the 50-day MA drops below the 200-day MA, signaling potential bearishness. While these crosses offer signals, they shouldn't be your sole decision-making tool. Instead, treat them as part of a broader strategy.

Now, when is the best time to act on these signals? The answer lies in the context of the broader market. For instance, during a strong uptrend, a golden cross might be an excellent opportunity to enter or add to a position. However, in a choppy or sideways market, the same signal might lead to false starts and whipsaws. Therefore, understanding the market environment is crucial, coupling crossovers with other indicators like volume or momentum oscillators to confirm the signal.

For day traders, moving average crossovers on shorter time frames can be invaluable. The combination of a 5-period and a 20-period moving average on a 15-minute or 1-hour chart can offer timely intraday signals. These are less reliable on their own due to the inherent noise in shorter time frames but can still provide an edge when used alongside other indicators like the Relative Strength Index (RSI) or MACD (Moving Average Convergence Divergence).

Crossovers can also help manage risk. Incorporating them into a trading plan can give a structured approach to stop-loss placement. For instance, if you're entering a long position based on a golden cross, a logical stop-loss might be just below the point where the short-term moving average crossed up. This allows you to manage downside risk effectively while giving your trade room to breathe.

Algorithmic traders or those employing automated systems can particularly benefit from MA crossovers. Coding moving average crossover strategies is relatively straightforward, and these strategies can be backtested with historical data to evaluate performance. However, discipline remains indispensable. Over-optimization or "curve-fitting" to historical data can lead to dismal performance in live markets. Always test your strategies across various market conditions to gauge their robustness.

There's also the matter of smoothing techniques. Exponential Moving Averages (EMAs) are often preferred over Simple Moving Averages (SMAs) because they give more weight to recent prices, making them more responsive. This responsiveness can be a double-edged sword; while faster to signal, EMAs are more susceptible to whipsaws. Hence, the choice between EMAs and SMAs becomes a personal one, depending on your trading style and tolerance for false signals.

Besides traditional golden and death crosses, traders might look to other crossover strategies tailored to specific trading goals. One such approach is the "triple moving average crossover," where the addition of a third, intermediate-term moving average adds another layer of confirmation. For instance, using the 10-day, 50-day, and 200-day moving averages together can provide a more nuanced view, helping to filter out false signals and ensure stronger trend confirmation.

Remember, though, moving averages and their crossovers work best in trending markets. During periods of high volatility or non-directional movement, relying on these indicators alone might prove challenging. That's why many traders use them in conjunction with other tools, such as trendlines or support and resistance levels, to better gauge market conditions.

Lastly, psychological and emotional discipline can't be overstated. It's easy to get caught up in the excitement of a crossover signal, but it's essential to stick to your trading plan and not act impulsively. Use crossovers as part of a holistic strategy, consider your risk management rules, and make decisions based on data and analysis rather than gut feelings.

In summary, mastering moving average crossovers involves understanding their mechanics, testing them against historical data, and integrating them into a broader strategy. Whether you're a novice or an experienced trader, incorporating these signals can help in timing your trades more accurately and enhancing your overall market approach. By combining the simplicity of moving averages with disciplined execution, you can improve your chance of making well-timed, informed trading decisions.

Chapter 6:
Momentum Indicators
and Oscillators

M omentum indicators and oscillators are indispensable tools that inject clarity and precision into a trader's arsenal. By leveraging these instruments, traders can gauge the speed and strength of price movements in the market, enhancing their ability to pinpoint trends and potential reversals. Stochastics and the Moving Average Convergence Divergence (MACD) are two leading momentum indicators that traders frequently rely on to measure market momentum and generate trading signals. Through understanding how to interpret divergences, traders can spot early warning signs that often precede significant price movements, enabling more disciplined decision-making. Incorporating these indicators into trading strategies helps navigate the market's ebbs and flows with greater confidence and foresight. Whether you're aiming for short-term gains or long-term investments, mastering momentum indicators and oscillators can significantly amplify your trading acumen.

Stochastics and MACD: Identifying Momentum

Understanding the forces driving market momentum is crucial for any trader aspiring to make smarter, more informed decisions. The Stochastic Oscillator and the Moving Average Convergence Divergence (MACD) are two powerful tools in this regard. The Stochastic Oscillator shines in its ability to pinpoint overbought and oversold conditions by tracking the closing price relative to the range over a set period. On the other hand, the MACD offers a visual and mathematical representation of momentum, highlighting both trend strength and direction through the interplay of moving averages. By combining these indicators, traders can gain a nuanced perspective on market moves, enhancing their ability to time entry and exit points with precision. Remaining vigilant to divergences and crossover signals from these tools can act as early warning systems, bolstering risk management and reinforcing trading strategies.

Divergences: The Early Warning System

Divergences can be an invaluable tool for traders and investors when assessing the potential future movements of the market. Identified through momentum indicators and oscillators, divergences provide a predictive element that informs traders of potential trend reversals. Exhaustive knowledge of divergences elevates one's trading acumen, helping not only in capitalizing on market opportunities but also in avoiding potential risks.

At its core, a divergence occurs when the direction of the price movement disagrees with the direction of an indicator. These discrepancies serve as early warning systems, alerting traders that the current trend might be weakening and that a reversal or significant pullback could be imminent. Divergences are particularly relevant in the context of momentum indicators such as the Moving Average Convergence Divergence (MACD) and stochastics.

There are two primary types of divergences: regular divergences and hidden divergences. Understanding the distinctions and applications of each type can reinforce one's trading strategy. Regular divergences signal potential reversals and are identified when the price makes a new high or low, but the indicator does not. For instance, if the price of a stock reaches a new high but the MACD forms a lower high, it indicates a bearish divergence, suggesting a potential downward trend reversal.

In contrast, hidden divergences indicate trend continuation. These are observed when the price fails to create a new high or low, while the indicator does. For example, during an uptrend, if the price makes a higher low but the MACD makes a lower low, it can signal a bullish hidden divergence, suggesting the current uptrend is likely to continue. Recognizing these nuances helps traders make more informed decisions about entering or exiting positions.

Implementation of divergences in trading must be approached with a healthy dose of caution. While divergences can offer valuable insights, they are most effective when used in conjunction with other technical analysis tools. A divergence on its own doesn't guarantee a trend reversal or continuation; it merely highlights potential. Therefore, traders should confirm signals from divergences with other indicators, trendlines, or support and resistance levels to increase the reliability of their predictions.

Beyond merely identifying divergences, it's crucial to consider the context within which they occur. For instance, divergences are more significant when they materialize during overbought or oversold conditions. In such scenarios, the market is due for a correction, and the divergence can serve as the catalyst for the impending shift. Indicators like stochastics and Relative Strength Index (RSI) help determine these conditions, reinforcing the validity of a divergence signal.

Moreover, the timeframe in which a divergence is identified plays a vital role. Divergences on longer time frames, such as daily or weekly charts, tend to be more reliable and carry more weight than those on shorter time frames like 5-minute or 15-minute charts. However, shorter time frame divergences can be useful for day traders looking to capitalize on intra-day price movements. Aligning the analysis across multiple time frames can offer a more comprehensive view and reinforce confidence in the trading decision.

For example, a bullish divergence on the daily chart confirmed by a similar pattern on the weekly chart provides a stronger case for a potential upward turn in the market. When these divergences are observed in conjunction with other corroborating signals, such as breaking above a key resistance level, the probability of a successful trade increases manifold.

Furthermore, it's essential not to ignore the psychological aspect of trading divergences. They require patience and discipline, two fundamental traits for any successful trader. Reacting prematurely to a divergence signal could lead to false entries and potential losses. Hence, waiting for confirmation and aligning divergences with overall market context can mitigate impulsive decisions. Patience often rewards traders with better entry points and increased profitability.

Another strategic advantage of divergences is their ability to help in setting more precise stop-loss levels. If a trader identifies a bearish divergence, they may set a stop-loss just above the recent high, minimizing potential loss if the market continues to rise. Similarly, in the case of a bullish divergence, a stop-loss can be placed just below the recent low, offering a calculated risk approach. Proper risk management is integral to successful trading, and divergences provide an added layer of sophistication to these strategies.

In addition to individual traders, algorithmic trading systems also harness divergences. Algorithms can scan multiple assets across various timeframes, zeroing in on divergences with speed and accuracy that manual trading can hardly match. By programming rules that incorporate divergences, along with other technical criteria, algorithmic traders can execute trades with precision, reducing human error and emotional bias.

Divergences present a reliable, early warning system that enables traders to anticipate market movements. However, their utility is maximized when integrated with a broader technical analysis framework and a disciplined approach to trading. Whether you are a seasoned trader or a novice, incorporate divergences into your toolkit. Learn to spot these inconsistencies between price and momentum indicators, confirm them through additional analysis, and enhance your trading outcomes. Successful trading is not about predicting every market move; it's about making informed decisions based on a confluence of evidence. Divergences, when correctly interpreted, are a potent part of that evidence.

Chapter 7:
Patterns and Breakouts

Understanding chart patterns and their predictive power can be your ticket to capturing significant market moves. Patterns like head and shoulders, double tops, and triangles act as visual representations of the battle between buyers and sellers, and they often signal key turning points. When combined with the concept of breakouts, where price bursts through support or resistance levels, these patterns can offer invaluable insight into potential future price action. Whether it's flags, pennants, or wedges, recognizing the formation and subsequent breakout can dramatically enhance your trading success. Sharpen your skills in identifying these setups, and you'll be better positioned to make informed decisions, manage risk, and ultimately, unlock new trading opportunities.

Chart Patterns and Their Predictive Power

Understanding chart patterns is crucial for any trader looking to harness the predictive power of technical analysis. Patterns are the graphical representation of price movements over time, revealing the psychology of market participants. Every price movement tells a story of human behavior – from fear and greed to hope and panic. Recognizing and interpreting these patterns can help traders anticipate future price direction, providing a tangible edge in the market.

One of the most common patterns traders encounter is the **Head and Shoulders** pattern. It consists of three peaks: a higher peak (the "head") between two lower peaks (the "shoulders"). This pattern typically indicates a reversal from an uptrend to a downtrend. When the price breaks below the "neckline" connecting the two shoulders' lows, it often signals the start of a bearish trend. Conversely, an inverse head and shoulders pattern suggests a potential bullish reversal.

Double tops and double bottoms are another set of reliable reversal patterns. The double top resembles the letter "M" and suggests a trend reversal from bullish to bearish. The price reaches a high, pulls back, makes another similar high, then declines again – breaking the support line formed by the trough. A double bottom, forming a "W" shape, is its bullish counterpart. When the price breaks above the resistance line connecting the two peaks, it often signals a trend reversal to the upside.

Aside from reversal patterns, various continuation patterns hint at the existing trend's persistence. Among the most notable are **flags and pennants**. Flags are small rectangles that slope against the prevailing trend, while pennants are small symmetrical triangles extending from a flagpole. Both suggest brief consolidation before the trend resumes.

Wedges, like flags and pennants, can denote both reversals and continuations depending on their direction. Rising wedges often appear in a bearish context, signaling a coming drop in price when the support line is breached. Falling wedges suggest future bullishness, particularly when the resistance line is broken to the upside. Recognizing the context in which these patterns appear is vital for their correct interpretation.

Triangles deserve special mention due to their frequent occurrence and diverse implications. There are three main types: ascending, descending, and symmetrical. An **ascending triangle** has a flat top and rising bottom, usually indicating a bullish sentiment. As the price gets squeezed higher, breaking the upper resistance prompts further upward movement. Conversely, a **descending triangle** with a flat bottom and descending top suggests bearish continuation. The breakdown below support generally confirms the next leg down. Symmetrical triangles, however, are neutral and could break out in either direction.

Patterns don't just stop at these familiar shapes. Studying historical data reveals an array of exotic formations, such as cups and handles or even complex formations like the diamond top. The **cup and handle** pattern, particularly, signifies a strong continuation signal in bullish markets. The "cup" forms a rounded base, followed by a short consolidation period – the "handle". An upward price breakout from this handle typically resumes the upward trend.

An essential takeaway for traders is the predictive nature of these patterns. They aren't foolproof but provide high-probability setups. The key is confirmation. Waiting for price action to confirm a pattern before entering a trade minimizes risk. For example, in a head and shoulders pattern, the actual signal to enter isn't formed until the neckline is broken with volume support.

Volume plays a pivotal role in confirming the validity of chart patterns. A pattern break accompanied by high volume significantly increases the likelihood of a true breakout, as it reflects strong market participation. Conversely, a breakout on low volume may indicate a false move, potentially trapping traders in unfavorable positions.

Seasoned traders often combine chart patterns with other technical tools to enhance prediction accuracy. Integrating moving averages, momentum indicators, or even Fibonacci retracements with chart patterns can provide additional confirmation and improve the robustness of trading signals. This confluence of factors decreases the chances of false signals and increases the trader's confidence in their positions.

There's value in backtesting and studying historical chart patterns. By analyzing how certain patterns performed in the past under various market conditions, traders can develop a nuanced understanding of their reliability. Backtesting offers valuable insights that can be applied to future trading decisions.

Pattern recognition isn't just a technical skill; it's an art. Each price movement reveals a small piece of a larger puzzle. Successful traders learn to piece these fragments together, developing a coherent picture of market sentiment. Over time, honing this skill helps traders anticipate market moves with greater precision, enhancing their decision-making prowess.

Trading isn't about predicting with absolute certainty but about playing probabilities. Chart patterns are tools to tilt these probabilities in your favor, offering a systematic approach to potentially gain an edge in the markets. Combining these patterns with effective risk management and psychological discipline forms the cornerstone of successful trading.

Embrace the journey of mastering chart patterns. Practice, refine, and combine them with other technical analysis elements. By doing so, you're not just reacting to market movements but proactively positioning yourself to capitalize on the predictable nature of market psychology.

Breakouts and Breakdowns: Capturing Significant Moves

Breakouts and breakdowns are pivotal moments in trading that signify potential significant price movements. When a price moves above a resistance level, we call it a breakout, which often hints at increased buying interest and a potential upward trend. Conversely, when a price falls below a support level, it's known as a breakdown, signaling possible increased selling pressure and a downward trend. To effectively capture these key moves, traders need to combine sharp technical analysis with prompt decision-making. Utilize volume confirmation, as it acts as a powerful validator of a true breakout or breakdown. Pay attention to the context provided by preceding price action—understanding the broader market environment can enhance your ability to discern whether these movements are sustainable or merely false signals. Remember, mastering the art of identifying and reacting to breakouts and breakdowns can significantly amplify your trading performance and financial success.

Flags, Pennants, and Wedges

These represent some of the most potent configurations within the realm of technical analysis. For traders and investors—whether seasoned or beginners—these patterns provide essential insights into potential market movements. Known for their reliability, understanding these patterns could significantly enhance your trading arsenal.

Let's start with flags. In a trending market, a flag usually signifies a period of consolidation following a sharp price movement, often referred to as the flagpole. The flag itself is typically a short-term price channel that moves counter to the prevailing trend. Imagine a steep rise followed by a modest decline; that's your classic bull flag. Conversely, a steep drop followed by a modest rise forms a bear flag. The key takeaway here is that flags are continuation patterns, often suggesting the trend will resume once the consolidation period concludes.

While flag patterns might seem straightforward, their correct identification is vital. Flags usually form over a period of one to three weeks. If the consolidation lasts longer, be wary, as it might be a different pattern altogether. Also, volume tends to decrease during the flag formation and should spike again as the price breaks out of the flag pattern, confirming the continuation of the trend.

Next up are <u>pennants</u>. Similar to flags, pennants are also continuation patterns. However, instead of forming a channel, a pennant takes the shape of a small symmetrical triangle. The flagpole in a pennant setup is the same—a sharp price move leading to the triangle's formation. This pattern appears as the market experiences a brief consolidation, with the highs and lows converging towards an apex.

Pennants are rapid formations, typically lasting from one to three weeks. The similarity to flags can complicate initial identification, but the key difference lies in the converging trendlines of a pennant as opposed to the parallel lines of a flag. Another crucial aspect of pennants is the volume behavior: a strong volume increase during the flagpole phase, subsiding during the consolidation, and surging again during the breakout. This surge in volume at the breakout is often a telltale sign that the prevailing trend is likely to continue.

Understanding flags and pennants can simplify your trading strategy, but <u>wedges</u> bring another nuanced layer to the table. Unlike flags and pennants, wedges can serve as both continuation and reversal patterns. They are identified by converging trendlines but tilted either upwards or downwards, counter to the direction of the breakout.

Two main types of wedges exist: rising wedges and falling wedges. A rising wedge is formed when the price makes higher highs and higher lows, but the breakout ultimately occurs in the opposite direction—downward. This pattern often signifies a bearish reversal in an uptrend but can also act as a continuation pattern in a downtrend. A falling wedge, conversely, forms lower lows and lower highs. It generally suggests a bullish reversal in a downtrend or a continuation of an uptrend.

Wedges typically take longer to form compared to flags and pennants, often developing over several weeks to a few months. Volume behavior in wedges isn't as predictable but can provide additional clues. Usually, volume decreases as the wedge forms and may increase slightly before the price breaks out. However, the volume usually surges after the breakout, confirming the new trend direction.

While identifying these patterns, always consider the broader market context. Are other technical indicators supporting the anticipated move? For instance, moving averages, momentum oscillators, and support and resistance levels can add layers of confirmation or signal potential false breakouts. It's about painting a holistic picture rather than relying on one standalone pattern.

Implementation is equally crucial. Spotting a flag, pennant, or wedge isn't enough; you need to act on it. This is where trade execution comes into play. Set your entry orders just above the high of the bull flag or pennant or just below the low of the bear flag. With wedges, entries should align with the anticipated breakout direction. Don't forget risk management. Always establish stop-loss orders to protect your capital if the market doesn't move as anticipated.

The beauty of mastering flags, pennants, and wedges lies in their ubiquity across different timeframes and markets. Whether you're a day trader seeking opportunities in an hourly chart or a swing trader focusing on daily and weekly charts, these patterns are universally applicable. They can be found in stocks, forex, commodities, and cryptocurrencies, making them indispensable tools in your trading toolkit.

Incorporating these patterns into algorithmic trading strategies is another frontier worth exploring. Algorithms can be designed to scan multiple markets simultaneously, identifying potential flag, pennant, and wedge formations. Backtesting these strategies against historical data can fine-tune their effectiveness and contribute to more robust, data-driven trading decisions.

To truly harness the power of these patterns, practice is crucial. Historical chart analysis can help you develop an eye for these formations and test your hypothesis regarding breakouts and volume changes. As you become more proficient, real-time charting will offer immediate opportunities, enhancing your ability to make quick, informed trading decisions.

In conclusion, flags, pennants, and wedges are irreplaceable components of technical analysis. They offer predictive insights into market behavior, helping traders capitalize on fleeting opportunities. By understanding these patterns and incorporating them into a broader trading strategy, you enhance your ability to read the market and make informed trading decisions. Keep practicing, stay disciplined, and these patterns can become powerful allies in your trading journey.

Chapter 8:
Candlesticks and Beyond

In this chapter, we'll dive deep into the world of candlestick patterns and their potent blend with other technical analysis tools to supercharge your trading prowess. Candlesticks, with their rich history and visual clarity, are like a trader's secret language, offering insights into market sentiment and potential price reversals. But don't stop there; the real magic happens when you combine these patterns with other indicators such as moving averages, volume, and trendlines. This amalgamation creates a robust analytical framework, enhancing accuracy in predicting market movements and managing risk more effectively. By mastering candlesticks and integrating them into a broader technical strategy, you not only gain a nuanced understanding of price action but also bolster your decision-making skills, empowering you to navigate the markets with confidence and precision.

The Language of Candlesticks

Candlesticks charting, a technique developed by rice traders in Japan centuries ago, is an indispensable tool in the toolkit of modern traders. Through a series of visual cues, candlesticks meticulously depict the emotions of market participants, capturing the intricate balance of fear, greed, optimism, and pessimism. To the untrained eye, these charts might appear as mere patterns or abstract shapes, but to the seasoned analyst, they're an eloquent manifestation of market psychology.

The most fundamental unit of a candlestick chart is, naturally, the candlestick itself. It comprises four key components: the open, high, low, and close prices within a given time frame. Each candlestick reflects a story of what transpired during that period—a narrative of the market's tug-of-war. The rectangular body (or real body) of the candlestick indicates the range between the open and close prices. When the close price is higher than the open, the body is typically colored or shaded differently compared to when the close is lower than the open. The lines extending from the body, known as shadows or wicks, signify the price extremes reached within that session.

Beyond the basic structure, candlesticks forge a language through a series of unique patterns. Single candlesticks are valuable, but their real power is unlocked when combined into patterns, each with its distinct meaning. Commonly recognized single candlestick patterns include the Doji, Hammer, and Shooting Star. The Doji, characterized by a body so narrow it's almost a line, indicates indecision in the market. This equal tug from both buyers and sellers suggests that a forthcoming shift or continuation in the trend may occur, depending on its context within the broader chart.

Multi-candlestick patterns are where the real storytelling begins. For instance, the Bullish Engulfing pattern, consisting of a small bearish candlestick followed by a larger bullish candlestick, signals a potential reversal of a downward trend. The larger bullish candlestick 'engulfs' the preceding bearish one, suggesting that buyers have overtaken sellers, thus pushing the price higher. This pattern can often be found at the bottom of a downtrend, serving as an optimistic indicator for traders eyeing long positions.

Conversely, the Bearish Engulfing pattern tells the opposite story—a bearish reversal. During an uptrend, if a smaller bullish candlestick is followed by a larger bearish one, it indicates that sellers have overpowered buyers, potentially precipitating a downtrend.

Recognizing these patterns allows traders to anticipate market moves rather than react to them, giving them a crucial edge.

Candlesticks also form a lexicon of shorter-term patterns, known as continuation and reversal patterns. Continuation patterns, like the Rising Three Methods, suggest that the prevailing trend is likely to continue. This particular pattern starts with a long bullish candlestick, followed by three smaller bearish candlesticks, and concludes with another large bullish candlestick. It illustrates that minor pullbacks within an overall uptrend shouldn't be misconstrued as a bearish reversal.

Reversal patterns, on the other hand, indicate potential changes in the direction of the trend. One notable example is the Morning Star pattern, a bullish reversal pattern seen at the bottom of downtrends. It comprises three candlesticks: the first is a long bearish candlestick, the second a small-bodied candlestick that gaps lower, and the third a long bullish candlestick that closes near the midpoint of the first candlestick. This pattern signals the weakening of bearish pressure and the potential for a bullish turnaround.

The real beauty of candlestick charting lies in its adaptability. While Western technical analysis might rely heavily on indicators like RSI or Bollinger Bands, candlestick patterns provide immediate and rich context. Integrating these patterns with other technical tools enhances their predictive power. For example, when a Bullish Engulfing pattern appears at a key support level, it carries more weight. This synergy allows for more sophisticated trading strategies and better risk management.

Understanding the language of candlesticks offers more than just a way to interpret price action; it builds a bridge to the underlying market sentiment. By paying close attention to the nuances of candlestick patterns, traders can gain invaluable insights into the prevailing psychology of market participants. Whether it's spotting a potential reversal or confirming a continuing trend, the ability to read, analyze, and interpret these patterns can make all the difference between success and failure in the trading world.

Candlestick analysis is not limited to individual stocks but applies to a variety of trading instruments, ranging from forex to futures and even cryptocurrencies. These versatile patterns can be applied across different time frames as well, allowing day traders and long-term investors alike to benefit from their insights. The adaptability and universal applicability make candlesticks an essential component of any trader's analytical arsenal.

Market volatility adds another layer of complexity to candlestick analysis, but also amplifies its utility. During periods of high volatility, candlestick patterns can act as beacons, guiding traders through the chaos. Recognizing patterns like the Spinning Top in such volatile markets can indicate periods of indecision, prompting traders to reassess their strategies and possibly take protective measures to mitigate risks.

The interpretation of candlestick patterns is as much an art as it is a science. Different traders may interpret the same pattern in differing ways, influenced by their trading styles, time horizons, and risk tolerances. This subjectivity, however, is what makes trading both challenging and exhilarating. It necessitates a dynamic approach, blending empirical analysis with intuitive decision-making.

It's crucial to avoid placing undue emphasis on isolated candlestick patterns. Instead, these patterns should be viewed as part of a broader analytical framework. Confirmation from other technical indicators, volume analysis, and overall market conditions should be sought to substantiate the signals derived from candlestick patterns. Properly contextualized, candlestick analysis can become a powerful predictive tool rather than a mere descriptive one.

Finally, your mastery over the language of candlesticks will grow with practice and experience. As you immerse yourself more in market data and various chart setups, you'll begin to internalize the subtleties and intricacies of these patterns. Much like learning a new language, fluency comes with time and exposure. Keep a trading journal to document your observations and insights related to candlestick patterns. Over time, this practice will deepen your understanding and enhance your analytical prowess.

In sum, candlestick charting offers a visually intuitive and comprehensive way to engage with market data. By learning to decode the language of candlesticks, traders can gain a significant edge, transforming raw price data into actionable insights. This language, rich in historical significance and rife with practical utility, remains as relevant today as it was centuries ago, continuing to illuminate the path for traders navigating the complex world of financial markets.

Combining Candlesticks with Other Technical Tools

Combining candlestick patterns with other technical analysis tools can significantly enhance a trader's accuracy and decision-making process. While candlesticks alone offer a visual representation of price action and potential reversals, pairing them with various indicators and methods forms a more robust trading strategy. By doing so, traders can confirm signals and mitigate risks, leading to more informed investment choices.

One effective way to integrate candlesticks with other tools is by using moving averages. Moving averages smooth out price data, creating a clearer picture of trend direction and strength. When a candlestick reversal pattern appears near a moving average, it frequently signifies a high-probability opportunity. For example, if a bullish engulfing pattern forms at the 50-day moving average, it may indicate the beginning of an upward trend. Conversely, a bearish engulfing pattern at the 200-day moving average could suggest an imminent decline.

Volume analysis also plays a crucial role when combined with candlestick patterns. Volume provides insight into the strength and conviction behind price movements. For instance, a rising volume accompanying a bullish candlestick pattern such as a hammer or a morning star is a stronger confirmation of an upward move. On the contrary, if a bearish pattern like a shooting star forms on high volume, it signals that sellers are overpowering buyers.

Another critical tool to consider is the Relative Strength Index (RSI). The RSI measures the speed and change of price movements, oscillating between 0 and 100. When combined with candlestick patterns, RSI can highlight overbought or oversold conditions. For example, a hammer within the RSI's oversold territory provides a compelling buy signal. Similarly, a doji near the overbought level of RSI might warn traders of a potential reversal.

Trendlines and channels offer yet another layer of analysis that can enhance the signals provided by candlesticks. Drawing trendlines connecting significant highs and lows can highlight support and resistance areas. When a candlestick pattern appears at these critical juncture points, it often confirms a change in trend. For example, a bullish piercing pattern near a rising trendline may indicate a continuation of the bullish trend, whereas a bearish engulfing pattern at a descending trendline might signal further decline.

Another invaluable tool is the Bollinger Bands. Bollinger Bands consist of a moving average and two standard deviations above and below it, encapsulating most of the price action. When combined with candlesticks, Bollinger Bands can indicate volatility and potential reversals. A candlestick pattern breaking the upper or lower band can signal overextension and a likely price reversal. If a bullish engulfing pattern coincides with the price touching the lower Bollinger Band, it could suggest an impending bullish move.

The MACD (Moving Average Convergence Divergence) is also a powerful tool when used alongside candlestick patterns. The MACD indicator highlights changes in momentum, helping traders spot potential buy or sell opportunities. A bullish crossover of the MACD line above the signal line, coupled with a bullish candlestick pattern like a morning star, can signal a strong buying opportunity. Conversely, a bearish crossover paired with a bearish pattern such as a dark cloud cover can represent a prime selling point.

Fibonacci retracement levels are another critical component that complement candlesticks. These levels highlight potential support and resistance zones based on the Fibonacci sequence. Candlestick patterns appearing near these Fibonacci levels often provide strong reversal signals. For instance, a bullish hammer forming around the 61.8% retracement level could be a robust indicator of a bullish rebound. Similarly, a bearish engulfing pattern near the 38.2% retracement level may forecast a downward movement.

Incorporating oscillators like the Stochastic Indicator adds another dimension to candlestick analysis. The Stochastic Oscillator measures the closing price relative to the price range over a specific period, oscillating between 0 and 100. When candlestick patterns and the Stochastic Oscillator align in overbought or oversold regions, the signals are particularly potent. A bullish reversal pattern such as a morning star in the oversold zone of the Stochastic Oscillator can strongly suggest an upward move. Correspondingly, a bearish candlestick pattern in the overbought region may predict a downward trend.

Additionally, incorporating the Average True Range (ATR) can prove beneficial. ATR measures market volatility by decomposing the entire range of an asset price for that period. When combined with candlestick patterns, ATR can help traders gauge the strength of a move. A significant candlestick pattern like the bullish engulfing pattern accompanied by a rising ATR could signify a strong potential rally. Conversely, a bearish pattern with increasing ATR may suggest a powerful downtrend.

Lastly, integrating sentiment analysis can add a fundamental dimension to candlestick and technical tool combinations. Sentiment indicators such as the Put/Call Ratio or the Fear and Greed Index gauge market emotions and psychology. For instance, a bullish candlestick pattern in an environment where sentiment indicators show extreme fear might indicate a market bottom and a potential buying opportunity. Conversely, a bearish candlestick in an environment of extreme greed could warn traders of impending corrections.

By weaving together these various technical tools with candlestick analysis, traders craft a multifaceted approach. This methodology doesn't just offer one-dimensional signals but rather a holistic view of the market, enhancing decision-making accuracy. As you develop your trading strategy, remember that no single tool is infallible. The strength lies in their combination, providing a more comprehensive understanding of market dynamics that can lead to more informed and potentially rewarding trading decisions.

Chapter 9:
Fibonacci and Gann Theory

Embracing the principles of Fibonacci and Gann Theory can significantly enhance a trader's toolkit by providing powerful methods for predicting price movements and identifying potential turning points in the market. At the heart of Fibonacci analysis lies the "golden ratio," a mathematical relationship that manifests in nature and financial markets alike, offering traders a way to identify key retracement and extension levels. Using Fibonacci retracements, traders can map out support and resistance levels that may indicate where a trend might pause or reverse. Conversely, Gann Theory introduces a unique approach by focusing on geometric angles and time cycles, allowing for a more structured analysis of price and time relationships. Gann's methods, like his signature angles, provide a scaffold to determine significant price movements based on time intervals. Combining these two theories, investors can gain a deeper understanding of market dynamics, refine their strategies, and potentially uncover trading opportunities that align with these natural laws. Ultimately, the integration of Fibonacci and Gann Theory empowers traders to make well-informed decisions, improving their chances of achieving success in the ever-complex world of financial markets.

Fibonacci Retracements and Extensions: The Golden Ratio

The allure of Fibonacci retracements and extensions lies in their foundation on a naturally occurring sequence, often referred to as the "Golden Ratio". This sequence is deeply ingrained in the natural world, from the spiraling patterns of galaxies to the structure of DNA. Traders and investors harness this mathematical elegance to identify key levels of support and resistance, aiming to enhance precision in their market decisions.

Fibonacci retracements are grounded in the concept that markets don't move in straight lines. After a significant price movement, whether bullish or bearish, markets often retrace a portion before resuming the initial trend. This temporary counter-trend movement can be vital for identifying potential entry and exit points. The key retracement levels typically used are 23.6%, 38.2%, 50%, 61.8%, and 78.6%. Each level represents a fraction of the primary move's length, calibrated against the Golden Ratio.

To calculate these retracement levels, begin by identifying the high and low of the foundational movement. For an uptrend, the low point serves as the base, while for a downtrend, the high point sets the limit. From these points, Fibonacci levels project horizontal lines at the specified percentages. These lines then assist traders in predicting where the price may halt its counter-trend move and resume the primary trend.

Understanding the psychology behind these levels is equally crucial. Traders and investors around the globe are aware of, and sometimes act on, Fibonacci levels, creating a self-fulfilling prophecy. When numerous market participants place their buy or sell orders around these levels, it amplifies the movement's validity, reinforcing its power.

On the flip side, Fibonacci extensions forecast potential price targets beyond the current trend, allowing traders to gauge how far a price may move following a retracement. The commonly used extension levels are 61.8%, 100%, 161.8%, 200%, and 261.8%. These levels emanate from the same principle but project beyond the trend rather than within it. Essentially, while retracements help in navigating towards potential corrective phases within a primary trend, extensions provide targets to anticipate where the trend could climax.

Consider a trader observing a stock that's just completed a significant upward movement from $100 to $150. Applying Fibonacci retracements requires plotting these levels on the chart from the $100 low (start of the move) to the $150 high (end of the move). The retracement levels would then appear at approximately $138.2 (23.6%), $130.9 (38.2%), $125 (50%), $119.1 (61.8%), and $108.5 (78.6%). If the stock begins to retrace, these levels offer potential support points to watch for a reversal back to the uptrend.

Extensions come into play when that stock starts rising again after hitting support. Taking the same $100 to $150 move, if the stock retraces to $130 and then rallies, traders might look at extensions to set profit targets. A 161.8% extension level would project the stock price to around $180.9, offering insight into potential resistance areas and market sentiment regarding the continuation of the trend.

It's essential to integrate these Fibonacci techniques with other technical indicators and analyses. Relying solely on Fibonacci can provide insights, but combining it with trend analysis, volume, or momentum indicators enhances the robustness of the predictions. This multi-faceted approach ensures traders are not blindsided by unforeseen market dynamics and maintain a holistic view of market conditions.

Trading requires adapting to real-time market shifts, and Fibonacci levels can act as a versatile tool in a trader's arsenal. They assist in identifying key levels to watch, but like any tool, their effectiveness increases when used in conjunction with a well-rounded strategy. This strategic implementation of Fibonacci principles can lead to more informed and confident trading decisions, increasing the probability of success.

The Golden Ratio also influences algorithmic trading systems. Incorporating Fibonacci retracements and extensions into algorithms enables automated systems to execute trades at strategic levels, devoid of emotional biases. These automated systems analyze volumes of data rapidly, continuously adjusting positions in response to price movements and key Fibonacci levels. This plays a significant role in today's high-frequency trading environments where speed and precision are paramount.

In summary, Fibonacci retracements and extensions extend beyond mere lines on a chart. They're embedded in the universal principles of balance and harmony, offering traders a structured approach to navigating market complexities. By integrating these concepts into your trading strategy, you tap into centuries-old wisdom, guided by the ever-present Golden Ratio.

Gann Angles: Time and Price Analysis

William Delbert Gann, a trader in the early 20th century, developed a unique set of techniques to analyze markets. These methods combined geometry, astronomy, and ancient mathematics. Gann believed that time and price move in tandem, creating specific angles that highlight potential market movements. His methods cannot guarantee success but mastering them can provide traders a new perspective on market behavior.

At the heart of Gann's methods are Gann angles, which are lines drawn at specific geometric angles on price charts. Among these, the 1x1, or 45-degree angle, is the most significant. This angle represents a balance between time and price, suggesting that one unit of time equals one unit of price. When prices move along this line, it signifies a stable trend. If prices break above or below, it indicates potential changes in market direction.

To effectively use Gann angles, traders must understand how to construct them correctly. Begin by identifying a significant low or high point on the chart. From this point, draw lines that move in specific ratios like 1x1, 2x1, 1x2, 3x1, etc. Each angle represents different levels of support and resistance, and these lines can help traders predict future price movements.

But why stop at just the 1x1 angle? Gann's work emphasized the importance of a series of angles to create a comprehensive view of the market. For instance, the 2x1 angle suggests that prices are rising at twice the rate of time, indicating a strong uptrend. Conversely, a 1x2 angle implies a slower price increase relative to time. These angles create a grid that can portray potential market trends accurately. Implementing multiple Gann angles on a single chart can highlight potential areas of price support and resistance, aiding in decision-making.

It's crucial to note that Gann angles must be adjusted based on the scaling of charts. Logarithmic scales are often preferred because they consider the percentage change in price rather than absolute values. This adjustment ensures that angles remain consistent and meaningful across various time frames. Without proper scaling, the true value of these angles might be lost.

Integration with time cycles further amplifies the utility of Gann angles. Gann believed that markets moved in predictable cycles and that specific time intervals, like 30, 60, or 90 days, were important in observing market trends. Combining these time cycles with Gann angles allows traders to create a predictive framework of when significant market moves might occur.

Traders can leverage Gann angles to identify areas of confluence, where multiple angles intersect. These intersections often represent strong support or resistance zones. When price action approaches these areas, it can provide traders with a high probability trading opportunity. For instance, if a price nears the intersection of a 1x1 and a 2x1 angle, it may signify a stronger likelihood of reversal or continuation, giving traders a clear signal on how to position their trades.

The concept of squaring time and price is another essential element of Gann theory. Squaring occurs when a unit of time matches a unit of price. For example, if a stock moves from $100 to $150 in 50 days, the move can be considered squared if a significant trend change occurs on or around the 50-day mark. Recognizing these squares helps traders forecast turning points more accurately.

Beyond simple trend analysis, Gann angles can help with more complex market situations. One of Gann's principles was that history tends to repeat itself. By analyzing historical price data using Gann angles, traders can identify repeating patterns that may emerge under similar market conditions. This historical analysis requires meticulous charting and observation, but the insights gained can be invaluable.

Gann angles also harmonize well with other technical analysis tools. For instance, combining them with Fibonacci retracements can create potent methods for identifying potential market reversals or continuation patterns. Gann angles provide the geometric framework, while Fibonacci levels give specific price targets. Together, they form a robust system for navigating volatile markets.

However, it's important to approach Gann angles with a realistic mindset. No technical tool is infallible, and Gann angles are no exception. Their effectiveness often depends on the skill and experience of the trader. Learning to apply Gann angles takes time and practice, and traders should start by experimenting on historical charts before applying these techniques in live trading.

Incorporating Gann angles into a broader trading plan is essential for achieving consistent results. These angles serve as one piece of the puzzle, complementing other indicators like moving averages, volume analysis, and momentum oscillators. By integrating various tools, traders can develop a well-rounded strategy that adapts to different market conditions.

In summary, Gann angles provide a unique lens through which to view market movements. They combine the elements of time and price in a geometrically structured manner, offering traders a disciplined approach to predict market trends. Although they require practice and careful application, understanding Gann angles can enhance traders' ability to make informed investment decisions.

Chapter 10:
Elliot Wave Theory
and Market Cycles

Elliot Wave Theory, a groundbreaking concept introduced by Ralph Nelson Elliot, dives deep into the cyclical nature of market movements and investor psychology. This theory essentially dissects market cycles into a series of predictable wave patterns—five wave impulses followed by three-wave corrections—that mirror the natural rhythm of financial markets. By understanding these wave patterns, traders can anticipate potential market turning points and make more strategic decisions. Elliot's insight suggests that markets move in fractals, creating a composite of waves that can offer foresight into future price actions. When combined with a keen analysis of market cycles, this approach empowers traders and investors with a tool for navigating the chaotic ebb and flow of the market, transforming complexity into clarity and enabling a strategic edge in financial forecasting.

Principles of the Elliot Wave Theory

The Elliot Wave Theory is a comprehensive method for analyzing market sentiment through waves, offering invaluable insights for traders and investors. Developed by Ralph Nelson Elliot in the 1930s, this theory is based on the idea that financial markets move in repetitive cycles or waves. According to Elliot, these cycles are influenced by the collective psychology of market participants, creating patterns that are observable and predictable.

At its core, Elliot Wave Theory consists of two main types of waves: impulsive and corrective. Impulsive waves, also known as motive waves, move in the direction of the prevailing trend. They are composed of five sub-waves, which are labeled 1, 2, 3, 4, and 5. Corrective waves, on the other hand, move against the prevailing trend and consist of three sub-waves labeled A, B, and C.

Understanding the specifics of these wave structures is critical, but it's equally essential to grasp the broader principles that govern them. The most fundamental principle of Elliot Wave Theory is that markets are fractal in nature. This means that the wave patterns repeat on different time scales, from long-term charts down to minute-by-minute price movements. This fractal nature allows traders to apply the principles of Elliot Wave Theory across various time frames, making it a versatile tool for both day traders and long-term investors.

Another key principle is the rule of alternation, which helps traders anticipate the future direction of the market by analyzing the structure of the corrective waves. For instance, if wave 2 of an impulsive wave is a sharp correction, wave 4 is likely to be a shallow correction, and vice versa. This interplay between impulsive and corrective waves enables traders to strategically position themselves within the market cycles.

Wave degree is another pivotal concept in Elliot Wave Theory. Waves are categorized into different degrees based on their time span and magnitude. These degrees range from Grand Supercycle waves, which can span several centuries, to Minuette and Subminuette waves that occur within minutes. Recognizing these varying degrees allows traders to zoom in and out of different market perspectives, aligning their strategies with both short-term movements and long-term trends.

Elliott also identified rules and guidelines that help delineate valid wave patterns. The most critical rules are:

- Wave 2 cannot retrace more than 100% of wave 1.

- Wave 3 cannot be the shortest wave among waves 1, 3, and 5.

- Wave 4 cannot overlap wave 1, except in the case of a diagonal triangle.

These seemingly simple rules provide a robust framework for analyzing market behavior and identifying potential entry and exit points.

One of the motivational aspects of using Elliot Wave Theory is the empowerment it provides to traders. By mastering these principles, traders can move away from trading based on gut feelings or hunches and start making decisions grounded in a systematic analysis of market cycles. This shifts their approach from reactive to proactive, fostering a trading environment that is both disciplined and strategically sound.

Moreover, the predictive power of Elliot Wave Theory can be inspiring. Being able to anticipate the next phase of market movement can boost confidence and improve decision-making. However, it's essential to combine Elliot Wave analysis with other technical indicators and sound risk management practices, ensuring a balanced and comprehensive trading strategy.

Corrective waves, although often considered less exciting than impulsive waves, are laden with opportunities. They typically unfold in one of three patterns: zigzag, flat, or triangle. Zigzags have a sharp, directional movement and can be highly profitable if identified correctly. Flats are more sideways or horizontal, reflecting a period of indecision or balance between buying and selling pressures. Triangles, often seen in the fourth wave of an impulsive cycle, signal consolidation before a final thrust in the direction of the trend.

One might wonder how Elliot Wave Theory fits into the modern trading environment dominated by algorithms and high-frequency trading. The principles of the Elliot Wave Theory remain relevant because at their heart, they capture human psychology and behavior, aspects that are unchanged regardless of technological advancements. Algorithms and trading systems are ultimately designed by humans and reflect collective behaviors and patterns, which align with the fractal nature of market cycles as described by Elliot.

Nevertheless, the key to effective utilization of Elliot Wave Theory lies in practice and experience. It's not merely about following the rules but learning to interpret the nuances of market waves. By applying Elliot Wave Theory, traders can decode the psychological phases of market participants: optimism, euphoria, anxiety, and despondency. This psychological insight can be an invaluable asset, allowing traders to see beyond the surface of price movements.

Additionally, practical application often involves a degree of subjectivity. Different traders might label waves slightly differently based on their interpretation of market data. Thus, it's crucial to approach Elliot Wave analysis as both a science and an art. Regularly reviewing historical wave patterns and practicing wave counts on various securities can sharpen one's skills and enhance the accuracy of future wave predictions.

The theory not only aids in identifying the current market position but also helps in determining potential future movements and market tops and bottoms, which are pivotal for making informed trading decisions. Recognizing where the market is within a cycle allows traders to anticipate reversals and capitalize on significant market movements.

Ultimately, mastering the principles of the Elliot Wave Theory requires dedication, study, and consistent application. By integrating these principles into your trading toolkit, you'll be more equipped to navigate the complexities of the markets, mitigate risks, and exploit opportunities to achieve your trading and investment goals. Just remember, while the Elliot Wave Theory is a powerful tool, its effectiveness is magnified when used in conjunction with other technical analysis techniques and sound risk management strategies.

Applying Elliot Waves to Market Cycles

When it comes to navigating the intricacies of the financial markets, utilizing the Elliot Wave Theory can be a game-changer. Understanding and effectively applying Elliot Waves to market cycles can provide traders and investors with a strategic edge, allowing for more informed decision-making and better timing. But how exactly does one go about integrating this theory into practical trading?

At its core, the Elliot Wave Theory posits that markets move in predictable, repetitive cycles based on investor sentiment and psychology. Named after Ralph Nelson Elliott, who discovered these wave patterns in the 1930s, the theory categorizes market movements into "waves" that form larger structures. The main waves you'll need to focus on are impulse waves and corrective waves, which together create a complete market cycle. Understanding these fundamental components enables traders to anticipate market movements and pivot strategies accordingly.

The market cycles can be dissected into five primary waves: three impulse waves (1, 3, and 5) and two corrective waves (2 and 4). Impulse waves move in the direction of the prevailing trend, while corrective waves move against it. When you look at a stock chart, the first wave (Wave 1) kicks off a new trend. This is usually followed by a corrective wave (Wave 2), after which Wave 3 often presents the most extended and robust trend move. Wave 4 brings another correction, and Wave 5 is the final push before a more significant market correction or reversal occurs.

So, how do you apply these waves in a real-world trading scenario? Start by identifying where you are within a particular cycle. This is easier said than done and requires both skill and experience. Wave counting, the act of identifying and labeling these waves on a chart, is a critical first step. You'll need to examine historical data, look for familiar patterns, and pay attention to other indicators that might validate your wave count. Tools like Fibonacci retracements can be incredibly helpful in identifying potential support and resistance levels, adding another layer of confirmation to your analysis.

It's essential to remember that Elliott Waves are fractal in nature. This means that you will see these patterns repeating on different timeframes, from hourly charts to monthly charts. By understanding the fractal nature, you can align your trading strategies to short-term and long-term perspectives, ensuring you're not missing out on broader trends or getting caught in market noise.

One of the common pitfalls is misidentifying the waves, especially in the initial phase. Beginner traders often find it challenging to distinguish between impulse and corrective waves. A practical tip here is to wait for completed wave patterns before making significant trading decisions. Patience is key. Always ask yourself: "Is this a corrective wave within a larger trend, or is it an entirely new impulsive wave in the opposite direction?" Utilizing multiple timeframes will provide clarity, allowing you to see the larger structure while honing in on smaller, actionable waves.

Applying Elliot Waves doesn't stop at just identifying the waves. You must also gauge the market sentiment and psychological factors at play. For instance, a strong Wave 3 usually signifies high investor confidence and participation, seen in increased volume and sharp price movements. Conversely, Wave 4 may signal caution and profit-taking activities, leading to a sideways or downward drift in prices.

Recognizing these behavioral cues will enhance your wave analysis, providing a more holistic market view.

Combining Elliot Waves with other technical indicators can elevate your trading strategy to the next level. For example, volume analysis can confirm the validity of a wave. Higher volumes during impulse waves and tapering volumes during corrective waves often underscore the wave's authenticity. Momentum indicators like the MACD or RSI might also provide clues about the market's state, such as identifying overbought or oversold conditions.

It's also crucial to set realistic expectations and manage risk effectively when trading on Elliot Waves. Since no theory or system is foolproof, incorporating risk management techniques, like stop-loss orders and position sizing, becomes vital. Always plan for scenarios where your wave count might be incorrect. This helps in mitigating potential losses and protecting your investment capital.

Wave extensions and truncations are other advanced concepts within the Elliot Wave Theory that traders need to be aware of. An extended wave is one where an impulse wave (usually Wave 3 or Wave 5) is longer than expected compared to the other waves, indicating extra momentum in the trend's direction. On the other hand, a truncated wave occurs when Wave 5 fails to go beyond the high point of Wave 3, often signaling a potential early reversal. Recognizing these deviations adds granularity to your market analysis.

While applying Elliot Waves may seem complex initially, consistent practice and experience will make the patterns clearer. Tools like Elliott Wave software or platforms with built-in analysis features can be incredibly beneficial for beginners. These tools can help automate wave counts, provide visual aids, and suggest potential wave scenarios, making the identification process more manageable.

Lastly, employing the Elliot Wave Theory should not be done in isolation. The best traders use it in conjunction with other market analysis techniques. Your trading plan can benefit immensely from integrating Elliot Waves with fundamental analysis, sentiment indicators, and real-world events. The more comprehensive your approach, the better your chances of navigating through the markets successfully.

In summary, applying Elliot Waves to market cycles offers traders a powerful tool to anticipate future market movements and make more informed trading decisions. The theory's real strength lies in its ability to give structure and predictability to seemingly chaotic market behaviors. By combining wave analysis with other technical indicators, continuously refining your skills, and practicing disciplined risk management, you can turn Elliot Wave Theory from a theoretical concept into an actionable trading strategy.

Chapter 11:
Trading Psychology and
Risk Management

In the fast-paced world of trading, your mindset is as crucial as your skillset. Trading psychology and risk management aren't just buzzwords; they're the cornerstone of sustainable trading success. Cultivating emotional discipline allows you to remain consistent, even when the market's volatility tempts you to abandon your strategy. Implementing robust risk management strategies—such as setting stop-losses and determining appropriate position sizes—ensures that no single trade can decimate your portfolio. Remember, the ultimate goal isn't just to make profits but to protect your capital so you can stay in the game for the long haul. By mastering the psychology of trading and adopting stringent risk management practices, you're not just surviving the market's whims; you're thriving and making informed, confident decisions.

Emotional Discipline: The Key to Consistency

Consistency in trading can be elusive, but emotional discipline is often the key that unlocks it. Many traders, no matter how experienced or knowledgeable, find themselves derailed by their emotions. Fear, greed, overconfidence—they all play a part in disrupting what could be a perfectly sound strategy. To maintain a steady hand, understanding and mastering your emotional responses is crucial.

First, let's recognize that emotions are natural. They're part of being human. Yet, the financial markets have a way of amplifying our deepest fears and desires. Picture this: you've done your analysis, and you're confident in your trade. But as soon as the market dips, panic sets in. Your heart races, and you're tempted to cut your losses prematurely. Instead of riding out the temporary downturn, you make a hasty decision. This is where emotional discipline comes in. It allows you to stick to your plan and make decisions based on logic, not emotions.

One powerful tool in cultivating emotional discipline is self-awareness. Knowing your triggers and patterns can help in developing strategies to counteract them. For instance, if you know you tend to panic when a trade goes against you, you can prepare by setting clear stop-loss orders. These act as a fail-safe, preventing you from making impulsive decisions. The key is to recognize the emotional impact of trading and put safeguards in place accordingly.

Another aspect of emotional discipline is patience. The most successful traders know that markets don't move according to their whims; they have their own rhythm and pace. Patience allows you to wait for the right setup and avoid jumping into trades just because you feel you should be doing something. This is easier said than done, especially in the fast-paced environment of day trading. But those who master this art often see better long-term results.

Building emotional discipline also involves setting realistic expectations. New traders, bursting with enthusiasm, often expect immediate success. When things don't go as planned, disappointment can cloud judgment. Understanding that losses are part of the game and that no strategy is foolproof helps in keeping a level head. By setting realistic expectations, you prepare yourself emotionally for the inevitable ups and downs of trading.

Moreover, having a structured trading plan can significantly aid in fostering emotional discipline. When you've outlined your entry and exit points, risk management strategies, and profit targets, you remove a significant amount of emotional decision-making. You're not relying on gut feeling in the heat of the moment; you're executing a well-thought-out plan. This structure can be a trader's best ally in maintaining discipline and ensuring consistency.

Let's not forget the importance of a healthy lifestyle in sustaining emotional discipline. Physical well-being has a direct impact on mental clarity and emotional stability. Regular exercise, a balanced diet, and adequate sleep can all contribute to a sharper, more disciplined mind. Traders often overlook these basic aspects, but they're essential. Trading requires intense focus and mental stamina, and a healthy body supports a healthy mind.

Mindfulness and meditation can also be incredibly beneficial in cultivating emotional discipline. Techniques such as deep breathing exercises and meditation can help in calming the mind and reducing stress. By integrating these practices into your daily routine, you build a reservoir of emotional resilience, making you less susceptible to the emotional rollercoaster of the markets.

Another valuable technique is visualization. Successful athletes often use this method to prepare for competitions, and traders can do the same. Visualize different trading scenarios and how you would react to them. This mental rehearsal can help in solidifying your emotional responses to various market conditions, making you more prepared and less reactive.

Finally, it's crucial to learn from your mistakes without being overly harsh on yourself. Every trader makes errors, but what separates successful traders from the rest is their ability to learn and adapt. Reviewing your trades, especially the ones that didn't go as planned, can offer invaluable insights. Understand what went wrong and how your emotions influenced your decisions. This reflective practice can foster a disciplined mindset and contribute to consistent performance.

In conclusion, emotional discipline is not just a concept; it's a vital skill that needs to be developed and honed continuously. It's about understanding your emotional triggers, preparing for them, and creating strategies to manage them. It's about patience, setting realistic expectations, and having a structured plan. It's about maintaining a healthy lifestyle, practicing mindfulness, and learning from mistakes. Each of these elements plays a role in helping you navigate the unpredictable waters of trading with a steady hand.

Emotional discipline is indeed the key to consistency in trading. When you master it, you'll find that the financial gains follow naturally. You'll be able to stick to your strategies, manage your risks effectively, and make decisions based on logic rather than emotion. This discipline not only enhances your trading performance but also brings a sense of fulfillment and confidence in your trading journey.

Remember, mastering emotional discipline is an ongoing process. It requires continuous effort, reflection, and refinement. But the payoff is immense. As you cultivate this skill, you'll find yourself becoming a more resilient, confident, and consistent trader.

So, embrace the journey of mastering your emotions. Develop the tools, practices, and mindset needed to maintain emotional discipline. With time and persistence, you'll unlock the key to consistency and achieve greater success in your trading endeavors.

Risk Management Strategies

Risk management is the cornerstone of successful trading, arming traders with the tools to protect their capital and maximize their potential for profit. One powerful strategy is diversification, which involves spreading investments across various assets to reduce exposure to any single market move. Equally crucial is the practice of setting stop-loss orders to cap potential losses—a disciplined approach that helps prevent emotional decision-making during market volatility. Position sizing is another essential technique; by adjusting the size of each trade based on overall portfolio risk, traders can mitigate the impact of any single adverse event. Additionally, using trailing stops can lock in profits while allowing for growth as trades move in a favorable direction. Effective risk management isn't just about minimizing losses; it's about creating a balanced strategy that aligns with your trading objectives and risk tolerance, ultimately supporting long-term success and confidence in your trading endeavors.

Stop-Losses and Position Sizing

These are two fundamental pillars of risk management that should never be overlooked by traders, regardless of their experience level. Understanding and implementing these strategies can mean the difference between consistent profits and devastating losses. This section dives deep into the principles behind stop-losses and position sizing, providing practical insights and actionable advice.

First, let's talk about stop-losses. A stop-loss is a pre-determined price at which you will exit a trade to prevent further losses. It's a crucial tool that acts as a safety net, shielding you from the unpredictable swings of the market. Establishing a stop-loss requires a delicate balance—setting it too close to your entry point could result in premature exits, while placing it too far away might expose you to substantial losses. The key is to strike a balance that aligns with your risk tolerance and trading strategy.

One of the most reliable methods for setting stop-loss levels involves using technical indicators. For example, placing a stop-loss just below a significant support level can offer a buffer against short-term market noise while still protecting your capital. Additionally, Average True Range (ATR) can be employed to determine a stop-loss distance that accommodates market volatility. The idea is to position your stop-loss at a level that makes it unlikely to be hit by ordinary market fluctuations, yet close enough to limit your downside risk.

Another approach to setting stop-losses is the percentage-based method, where a trader decides to exit a position once it loses a certain percentage of its initial value. This method is straightforward and ensures that your risk per trade is consistent. For instance, you might decide not to risk more than 1-2% of your trading capital on any single trade. If you have $50,000 in your trading account, you would therefore not risk more than $500 to $1,000 per trade. This approach ensures that a series of losses won't wipe out your account.

To further illustrate the importance of stop-losses, consider the psychological benefits. Trading can be an emotionally taxing endeavor, and having a stop-loss in place helps manage these emotions by removing the constant anxiety of watching the market. It automates the decision-making process, allowing you to focus on identifying new opportunities rather than worrying about existing positions.

Position sizing refers to deciding how much capital to allocate to a single trade. Proper position sizing is imperative for managing risk and ensuring the longevity of your trading career. It goes hand-in-hand with stop-loss strategies because while a stop-loss controls how much you lose on a trade, position sizing controls how much you have at stake in the first place.

Several methods exist for determining position size. One popular approach is the fixed dollar amount method, where you decide on a fixed amount of money to invest in each trade. While simple, this method doesn't take into account the varying levels of risk associated with different trades. A more sophisticated approach is the use of the percentage of equity method, in which you allocate a fixed percentage of your trading capital to each trade. This method dynamically adjusts your position size as your account balance changes, providing a scalable way to manage risk.

One of the more advanced position sizing methods is the risk-based approach, which considers both the size of the stop-loss and your total trading capital. For example, if you decide to risk 1% of your capital on a trade and have a $10,000 account, you'd be risking $100. If your stop-loss is placed $2 away from your entry price, you would purchase 50 shares (because $100/$2 = 50). This method ensures that each trade represents a similar level of risk, making it easier to manage your overall portfolio risk.

Position sizing can also be adapted based on the volatility of the asset being traded. Assets with high volatility might warrant smaller position sizes to mitigate risk, whereas more stable assets could allow for larger positions. By incorporating volatility into your position sizing calculations, you can ensure that you are taking uniform risk across different assets, harmonizing your risk management strategy.

We've touched upon the mechanics, but let's not forget the psychological angle. Proper position sizing keeps you from putting too much on the line, thereby reducing stress and emotional decision-making. Trading larger positions than you're comfortable with can lead to panic selling or holding onto losing trades for too long. By adhering to a well-thought-out position sizing strategy, you maintain emotional equilibrium, making it easier to follow your trading plan.

For illustrative purposes, let's consider a real-world example. Imagine you have a $20,000 trading account and you decide to risk 1% of your capital on each trade. You identify a trading opportunity on Stock XYZ, with an entry point at $100 and a stop-loss at $95. This means you are willing to risk $5 per share. With your 1% risk allowance, which equals $200 in this case, you would buy 40 shares ($200/$5). If the trade goes against you, the maximum you stand to lose is $200, preserving your capital for future trades.

If you adhere to these principles, even a series of losses won't decimate your account. For instance, if you face five consecutive losing trades, each losing $200, you will still have preserved 95% of your original capital. This structured approach allows you to endure inevitable losing streaks without significant damage to your trading account.

It's crucial to combine stop-losses and position sizing with a holistic risk management strategy. This involves diversifying your trades across different assets and markets to spread your risk. A well-diversified portfolio is less likely to suffer large losses because it's not overly exposed to the fluctuations of any single asset or market segment. Always remember that no single trade should define your trading career; rather, it's the cumulative effect of all your trades that will determine your success.

While the idea of losing money is never pleasant, embracing the concept of stop-losses and position sizing helps traders shift their mindset from chasing profits to managing risk. This psychological shift is paramount for long-term success in trading. It allows you to approach the markets with a more analytical and less emotional perspective, enabling you to make clearer and more rational decisions.

In conclusion, mastering **Stop-Losses and Position Sizing** is indispensable for anyone serious about trading. These strategies provide a robust framework for managing risk, preserving capital, and enhancing your trading performance. By implementing disciplined stop-losses and thoughtful position sizing, you set yourself up for sustained success, ready to tackle the market's challenges with confidence and resilience. Remember, it's not just about making money; it's about protecting what you have to live to trade another day.

Chapter 12:
Developing a Trading Plan

Creating a solid trading plan is the cornerstone of any successful trading strategy, guiding your decisions in the heat of the moment and keeping emotional pitfalls at bay. First, it's crucial to build a rule-based trading system, defining specific entry and exit points grounded in technical indicators you've mastered. Evaluate these rules by backtesting over historical data to gauge their reliability. Performance metrics will help refine your approach, identifying strengths and weaknesses. Equally important is maintaining a trading journal, meticulously recording each trade, noting the strategy, emotions involved, and outcomes. This journal serves as a powerful feedback mechanism to enhance your methods continually. A disciplined trading plan isn't just about strategy; it's about fostering consistency and precision, ensuring your decisions are driven by logic, not impulse.

Building a Rule-Based Trading System

So you've delved into understanding market trends, interpreted volume and volatility, mastered moving averages, and harnessed the power of technical indicators. Now, it's time to channel all that knowledge into a structured, actionable, and rule-based trading system.

Developing a rule-based trading system isn't just about picking the right indicators; it's about creating a methodical approach that eliminates emotional biases. Emotions can cloud judgment, leading to irrational decisions that deviate from the overall trading plan. A rule-based system acts as a safeguard against these pitfalls and provides a clear framework to follow, ensuring consistency and discipline.

First, define the objectives of your trading system. Are you looking for steady, incremental profits, or are you hunting for big wins? This will determine the nature of the rules you'll set. Focus on achievable goals, such as a certain percentage of returns per month or quarter, and specify the level of risk you are willing to tolerate.

Your trading rules should cover entry and exit criteria. For instance, if you're using a moving average crossover strategy, specify which moving averages you're using and what constitutes a valid crossover. Consider setting up rules for different market conditions. For example, you could have one set of rules for trending markets and another for ranging markets. This helps you adapt to various market environments while maintaining a structured approach.

Next, incorporate risk management into your rule-based system. Determine how much of your trading capital you're willing to risk on each trade. This includes setting stop-loss levels, which are critical for limiting potential losses. A general rule of thumb is to risk no more than 1-2% of your capital on a single trade. Position sizing is equally important. Calculate the number of shares or contracts to trade based on your risk per trade and the distance to your stop-loss level.

Your trading rules should also include criteria for scaling in and out of positions. Scaling involves adjusting position sizes based on changing market conditions. For example, you can add to your position as the trade moves in your favor, or you can reduce your position size if the market shows signs of reversal. This flexible approach can help you maximize profits while minimizing exposure to adverse price movements.

Having a set of predefined rules for taking profits is essential. Define specific profit-taking levels, such as price targets or trailing stops. Price targets can be based on technical levels like support and resistance, or they can be determined by a fixed risk-to-reward ratio. Trailing stops allow you to lock in profits as the trade moves in your favor, by adjusting your stop-loss level to follow the market price.

Consistent evaluation and adjustment of your trading system are key to long-term success. Markets evolve, and so should your rules. Regularly review your performance and identify any patterns or anomalies. Keep a trading journal to document your trades, including the rationale behind each trade, the outcome, and any lessons learned. This can provide valuable insights into your system's strengths and weaknesses.

Backtesting is a crucial step before implementing any rule-based trading system. Use historical market data to test your rules and see how they would have performed in various market conditions. This can help you identify potential issues and fine-tune your system before risking real capital. While backtesting can provide valuable information, remember that past performance is not necessarily indicative of future results. Real-time testing with a small portion of your capital can help validate your system under current market conditions.

Once you've developed and tested your rule-based trading system, it's time to go live. Start with a small portion of your trading capital to gain confidence and experience with your system. Gradually increase your position sizes as you become more comfortable and confident in your rules. Stay disciplined and stick to your rules, even when emotions and market noise tempt you to deviate.

To ensure your rule-based trading system remains effective over time, stay informed about market developments and continuously educate yourself. Market conditions are constantly changing, and staying ahead of the curve is essential for maintaining a profitable trading strategy. Join trading communities, attend webinars, and read industry publications to stay updated on the latest market trends and technical analysis techniques.

Finally, remember that no trading system is foolproof. There will be periods of drawdowns and losses. The key to long-term success is to remain disciplined, follow your rules, and continuously refine your approach. By building a robust rule-based trading system, you can efficiently navigate the markets and make informed, rational decisions that align with your overall trading plan.

Backtesting and Evaluating Performance

Developing a trading plan doesn't end at theoretical frameworks; it requires a rigorous process of backtesting and performance evaluation. Backtesting involves applying your trading system to historical data to see how it would have performed in real market conditions. This process helps in identifying the strengths and weaknesses of your strategy, providing a clear picture of its reliability and potential profitability. By scrutinizing performance metrics such as return-on-investment (ROI), drawdowns, and win-to-loss ratios, traders can fine-tune their approach to mitigate risks and maximize gains. Effective backtesting ensures that your strategy isn't merely built on paper but is robust enough to handle the ebbs and flows of actual trading scenarios. Evaluating performance should be a continuous endeavor, allowing you to adapt and evolve your trading plan with changing market dynamics, thereby enhancing decision-making skills and fostering long-term success in your financial pursuits.

The Importance of Keeping a Trading Journal

The importance of keeping a journal cannot be overstated. A trading journal is much more than a simple log of your trades; it's an essential tool for continuous improvement and refinement of your trading strategy. It serves as both a mirror and a roadmap—reflecting your trading decisions, emotions, and outcomes while guiding you toward more informed and disciplined trading practices.

One of the primary benefits of maintaining a trading journal is that it offers invaluable insights into your trading behavior. By meticulously recording each trade, including the rationale behind it, the strategies used, and the market conditions at the time, you create a comprehensive database of your trading activities. This detailed record allows you to analyze your performance over time, identifying patterns in your success and failures. More importantly, it helps you recognize recurring mistakes, providing an opportunity to adapt and refine your methods to avoid those pitfalls in the future.

A trading journal also serves as a powerful tool for enhancing emotional discipline. Trading can be an emotional rollercoaster, with the potential to impact your decision-making process. Emotional reactions such as fear and greed can often lead to impulsive trades, overriding logical strategies. By documenting your emotional state before, during, and after each trade, you can gain a better understanding of how emotions influence your trading decisions. This self-awareness is critical in developing the psychological resilience necessary for consistent profitability.

While tracking quantitative metrics like profits, losses, and risk-to-reward ratios are essential, your journal should also include qualitative data. Note down observations about market conditions, news events, and personal reflections on each trade. Over time, this combination of quantitative and qualitative data paints a clearer picture of your trading environment and your reactions to it. Such comprehensive tracking enables more precise adjustments to your trading strategies, enhancing overall performance.

Incorporating a post-trade analysis section in your journal is equally critical. After a trade is closed, spend time reflecting on whether it adhered to your trading plan and rules. Document any deviations and understand the reasons behind them. Were you following a signal from a moving average crossover, or did you act on a hunch influenced by market sentiment? This post-mortem analysis sheds light on your judgment and helps you discern between disciplined trading and impulsive decisions.

Moreover, a well-maintained trading journal can reveal the effectiveness of your trading plan over different market conditions. Markets are dynamic, with varying levels of volatility and trends. By reviewing your journal, you can determine how well your strategies have performed during bullish, bearish, and sideways markets. This insight enables you to tweak your trading rules and strategies to better align with different market environments, thus enhancing your adaptability and robustness as a trader.

Consistency is a core principle in trading, and a trading journal enforces it. By diligently documenting every trade, you create a sense of accountability. It becomes harder to stray from your trading plan when you know that every action will be scrutinized later. This systematic approach fosters disciplined trading habits, which are crucial for long-term success.

Another significant advantage of maintaining a trading journal is its role in reinforcing risk management strategies. Effective risk management is the bedrock of any successful trading plan. Your journal should record the specifics of your risk management tactics for each trade, including position sizes, stop-loss levels, and risk-to-reward ratios. This detailed log helps ensure that you consistently apply your risk management rules, protecting your capital from undue risk exposure.

Additionally, a trading journal can assist in setting realistic performance goals. Documenting your trade results and thoughts helps in establishing a performance benchmark. By periodically reviewing your journal, you can assess whether you are on track to achieve your goals or if adjustments need to be made. This continuous feedback loop is vital for staying focused and motivated.

Consider the journal as your personal trading mentor. It provides objective feedback, something very few other tools can offer. While market professionals and seasoned traders often advocate for trading journals, the true value of this practice becomes evident only when one experiences its benefits firsthand. The continuous learning derived from journaling can be the difference between mediocrity and mastery in trading.

For those incorporating algorithmic or systematic trading into their strategies, a trading journal becomes even more critical. Algorithmic trading involves extensive backtesting and performance analysis. By maintaining a detailed log of algorithmic trades, traders can validate the performance of their trading algorithms in live markets against historical data. This real-time validation is essential for ensuring the robustness and effectiveness of automated trading strategies.

A well-kept trading journal also serves as a reservoir of knowledge for future reference. As market conditions evolve, strategies that worked well in the past may need to be revisited and adapted. Your journal provides a record of past decisions and their outcomes, offering a repository of strategies and lessons learned that can be leveraged in the future. This historical perspective can be invaluable during market shifts or when developing new trading approaches.

To make the journaling process more effective and less cumbersome, leverage modern technology. Several digital platforms and tools are designed specifically for traders, offering features that allow you to track trades, analyze performance, and generate reports. These tools can automate data entry for trade metrics, making it easier to focus on the qualitative aspects and insights of your trades.

Finally, the importance of regularly reviewing your journal cannot be overstressed. A trading journal is not a "set it and forget it" tool; its true power lies in consistent review and reflection. Set aside dedicated time each week or month to analyze your trades, catch up on your observations, and make necessary adjustments to your trading plan. This regular review process helps in reinforcing learning and ensures that you remain aligned with your trading goals.

To sum up, maintaining a trading journal is a discipline that embodies the essence of continuous improvement. It helps you understand your trading behavior, enhance emotional discipline, refine strategies, and manage risks effectively. In a realm as dynamic and challenging as trading, where both skill and psychology play pivotal roles, a trading journal can be your most valuable partner in achieving sustained success.

Online Review Request for This Book

If you've found value in "Developing a Trading Plan" and the rest of the book, please take a moment to leave an online review to help other traders discover these essential strategies and tools. Your feedback really matters!

Charting
a Path Forward in the Markets

As we close the book on our deep dive into the world of technical analysis, it's vital to realize that this isn't the end—it's merely the beginning. The knowledge you now possess provides a framework, but the future of your trading journey lies in the practical application and continual refinement of these concepts.

Technical analysis isn't a one-size-fits-all solution. Instead, think of the techniques and tools we've explored as parts of a vast toolkit. Your success hinges on your ability to select and adapt these tools according to the unique circumstances of each market scenario. Whether you're a day trader, a swing trader, or a long-term investor, your approach will be tailored by the specific aims and guidelines you've set.

Remember, the market is a living entity, shaped by countless factors including economic data, geopolitical tensions, and evolving trader psychology. This means the strategies that work today might need adjustment tomorrow. Flexibility and resilience are key to staying relevant and profitable in such a dynamic environment.

One of the fundamental pillars of lasting success in trading is continuous education. Staying abreast of new trends, tools, and techniques in the world of technical analysis is crucial. Subscribing to financial journals, participating in trading forums, and attending seminars can enhance your market knowledge and keep your strategies sharp.

Emotional discipline can't be overstated. Emotion-driven decisions often lead to regretful outcomes, as we saw in our section on trading psychology. Cultivating a mindset that prioritizes unemotional, rule-based decisions not only preserves your capital but also fosters long-term growth. Techniques such as journaling your trades and regular self-assessment can help in maintaining emotional equilibrium.

Your path forward will also be significantly influenced by how well you manage risk. Defaulting to conservative risk management strategies can provide a safety net that allows you to take calculated risks without jeopardizing your financial health. Don't just rely on stop-losses and position sizing; continually reassess your risk exposure based on market conditions and your own capital capacity.

Another powerful ally in your trading journey is the incorporation of backtesting and performance evaluation. Knowing how your strategies fare under different market conditions offers invaluable insights that can inform adjustments and enhancements. Analytical tools and software that aid in backtesting should be a staple in your trading toolkit. Their use helps in validating your strategies, thus boosting your confidence in deploying them in real-world scenarios.

Let's also talk about community. Involvement in trading communities can act as a support system, offering new perspectives and strategies you might not have considered. Engaging with like-minded individuals provides a platform for exchanging ideas, troubleshooting problems, and celebrating wins, no matter how small. It's an ecosystem where collective wisdom can significantly benefit individual growth.

While this guide has armed you with substantial knowledge, the journey doesn't stop here. The discipline of maintaining a trading journal, analyzing your decisions, and learning from both your successes and mistakes is a lifelong commitment. Such disciplined practices help in recognizing patterns in your behavior and adapting accordingly, thus paving the way for continuous improvement.

Moreover, with advancements in technology, the landscape of trading is continually evolving. Algorithmic trading, artificial intelligence, and machine learning are redefining technical analysis. Staying informed about these developments can offer competitive advantages, allowing you to innovate and refine your strategies.

In summary, charting a path forward in the markets involves a blend of theory, practice, emotion, and continual learning. It's about building a robust, adaptable strategy that aligns with your individual goals and comfort level. Embrace the challenges as opportunities for growth, and always strive for improvement. The markets will test your resolve, but armed with the knowledge from this book and a disciplined approach, you are well-prepared to navigate these complexities.

May your journey be marked by informed decisions, calculated risks, and the resilience to adapt and thrive in the ever-changing landscape of financial markets.

To your success and prosperous trading!

Glossary
of Technical Analysis Terms

Welcome to the "Glossary of Technical Analysis Terms." This section is devoted to defining and explaining key terms that traders, investors, and market enthusiasts frequently encounter. By familiarizing yourself with these terms, you'll be better equipped to understand market mechanics, interpret trading signals, and utilize various analytical tools.

Ask Price

The price at which a seller is willing to sell a security. In trading, it represents the lowest price a seller will accept to sell a stock or another type of asset.

Bid Price

The price at which a buyer is willing to purchase a security. It indicates the maximum amount a buyer is ready to pay for a stock or asset.

Bollinger Bands

A volatility indicator that consists of a set of three lines—a simple moving average (middle band) and two standard deviations (upper and lower bands). These bands expand and contract based on market volatility.

Bull Market

A market condition characterized by rising prices and generally positive investor sentiment.

Bear Market

A market condition characterized by falling prices and generally negative investor sentiment.

Breakout

The movement of a security's price above a resistance level or below a support level. This movement often indicates the likelihood of continuing in the same direction.

Candlestick Chart

A type of financial chart used to describe price movements of a security, derivative, or currency. Each "candlestick" typically shows four price points: open, close, high, and low.

Consolidation

A period of range-bound activity after a significant price movement, characterized by indecision in the market.

Correction

A short-term decline in stock prices following a prolonged period of upward movement. Typically, corrections are seen as healthy market adjustments.

Divergence

A situation where the price of a security and a technical indicator move in opposite directions. Divergences can signal potential reversals.

Exponential Moving Average (EMA)

A type of moving average that places a greater weight on the most recent data points. This makes it more responsive to new information compared to the Simple Moving Average (SMA).

Fibonacci Retracement

A tool used to identify potential support and resistance levels based on key Fibonacci ratios (23.6%, 38.2%, 50%, 61.8%, and 100%). Traders use these levels to predict the extent of a pullback.

Head and Shoulders Pattern

A reversal pattern that signals the end of a trend. It consists of three peaks: a higher peak (head) between two lower peaks (shoulders).

Moving Average Convergence Divergence (MACD)

A momentum oscillator that calculates the difference between two moving averages (typically the 12-day and 26-day EMAs), and then applies a 9-day EMA to this difference (signal line).

Relative Strength Index (RSI)

A momentum oscillator that measures the speed and change of price movements. It's typically used to identify overbought or oversold conditions, using a scale from 0 to 100.

Resistance

A price level where an uptrend can pause due to a concentration of selling interest. Essentially, it's a level where selling pressures overcome buying pressures.

Support

A price level where a downtrend can pause due to a concentration of buying interest. It's a level where buying pressures overcome selling pressures.

Trendline

A straight line connecting two or more price points and then extending into the future to act as a line of support or resistance.

Volume

The number of shares or contracts traded in a security or market during a given period. Volume is an important indicator in technical analysis as it provides insights into the strength of a price movement.

Volatility

The degree of variation of a trading price series over time, usually measured by the standard deviation of returns. High volatility indicates a high degree of risk, whereas low volatility signals a more stable asset.

This glossary aims to clarify some of the foundational terms used in technical analysis, providing a handy reference as you navigate through the book. Keep these definitions at your fingertips for quick consultation, and deepen your understanding as you explore more advanced concepts and strategies.

Appendix A: Resources and Tools for Technical Traders

In the fast-paced world of trading, having the right resources and tools can make all the difference between success and failure. This appendix provides a comprehensive list of key resources and tools that will empower technical traders to make informed decisions. Whether you're a seasoned analyst or a budding market enthusiast, these resources will enhance your trading toolkit.

1. Charting Platforms

Charting platforms are indispensable for any technical trader. These platforms provide access to real-time price data, various chart types, and a plethora of indicators.

- **TradingView** – Known for its user-friendly interface, TradingView offers a wide range of charts, social networking features, and a large library of custom scripts.

- **MetaTrader 4/5** – Popular among forex traders, MetaTrader offers advanced charting tools, automated trading capabilities, and access to a multitude of markets.

- **ThinkorSwim** – Offered by TD Ameritrade, ThinkorSwim is rich in features like real-time data, advanced charting tools, and paper trading options.

2. Data Providers

Reliable data is crucial for accurate analysis. These providers offer historical and real-time market data.

- **Bloomberg Terminal** – A professional service providing financial data, news, and analytics globally.

- **Thomson Reuters Eikon** – Offers similar services to Bloomberg, with comprehensive data and powerful analytics.

- **Yahoo Finance** – A popular free option for retail traders providing basic financial data and news.

3. News and Information Sources

Staying informed about market news, economic indicators, and developments is vital.

- **Reuters** – Provides real-time news and analysis on financial markets, politics, and more.

- **Bloomberg** – Known for its in-depth financial analysis and news coverage.

- **CNBC** – Offers live market news, analysis, and expert opinions.

4. Trading Journals

Maintaining a trading journal helps track performance and identify patterns in trading behavior.

- **Edgewonk** – A digital trading journal that allows you to analyze your trades, improve strategies, and manage risk.

- **TradingDiary Pro** – A comprehensive solution for tracking and analyzing trading performance.

5. Educational Resources

Continuous learning is essential for staying ahead in the market. These resources offer valuable educational content.

- **Investopedia** – Provides a wealth of articles, tutorials, and courses on various financial topics.

- **Coursera** – Includes courses on finance, trading, and technical analysis from top universities.

- **BabyPips** – Specializes in forex education with guides, forums, and trading tools.

6. Analytical Tools and Software

Advanced analytical tools can enhance decision-making by offering deeper insights and precise calculations.

- **Excel** – Useful for custom analytical models, scenario analysis, and data organization.

- **Python** – An essential programming language for algorithmic trading and data analysis.

- **MATLAB** – Provides powerful tools for numerical computation, visualization, and algorithm development.

7. Algorithmic Trading Platforms

Algorithmic trading platforms allow traders to create, test, and deploy automated trading strategies.

- **QuantConnect** – An open-source platform supporting multiple languages like Python and C#.

- **MetaTrader 5** – In addition to charting, it supports algorithmic trading with MQL5 programming language.

- **AlgoTrader** – Offers a robust infrastructure for institutional-grade algorithmic trading.

8. Brokerages

Choosing the right brokerage is crucial for executing trades efficiently. Look for features like low fees, high-quality customer service, and robust trading platforms.

- **Interactive Brokers** – Known for its low commissions, extensive market access, and advanced trading tools.

- **Charles Schwab** – Offers a range of investment options, user-friendly platforms, and strong customer support.

- **Robinhood** – Provides commission-free trading with an easy-to-use mobile app, ideal for beginners.

Final Thoughts

Arming yourself with the right resources and tools is a vital step in the journey of becoming a skilled technical trader. From state-of-the-art charting platforms to insightful educational resources, having these tools at your disposal will enable you to navigate the complexities of the market with greater confidence and precision. Keep exploring, stay informed, and never stop learning.

Appendix B:
Key Historical
Market Case Studies

In the vast ocean of market data, key historical case studies serve as lighthouses, guiding traders and investors towards better decision-making. These moments of extraordinary market behavior are more than just anecdotes; they're treasure troves of learning. By analyzing these pivotal events, we can uncover patterns, validate theories, and refine our trading strategies. Let's dive into some of the most significant market case studies that have shaped the landscape of technical analysis and trading.

The Crash of 1929

Nothing exemplifies market volatility quite like the Great Depression. The crash of October 1929 brought an end to the Roaring Twenties, a decade characterized by unprecedented economic prosperity and market exuberance. The Dow Jones Industrial Average plummeted nearly 25% over two days, a cataclysmic event that ushered in a decade-long economic slump.

From a technical perspective, the crash revealed the importance of recognizing overbought conditions and the perils of excessive leverage. Chart patterns such as head and shoulders formations and double tops, which signaled potential reversals leading up to the crash, were either ignored or underestimated by many. The ensuing bear market highlighted the vital role of risk management and stop-loss orders in preserving capital.

The Dot-com Bubble

The late 1990s and early 2000s were a thrilling time for technology stocks, culminating in the dot-com bubble. During this period, the NASDAQ Composite index soared as internet-based companies' valuations skyrocketed purely on speculation and hype. The bubble burst in March 2000, and by 2002, the NASDAQ had lost approximately 78% of its peak value.

In hindsight, several indicators signaled the bubble's collapse. Dramatic increases in trading volume and euphoric market sentiment were red flags. Technical analysts noted the divergence between the rising prices and declining volume in many stocks, a classical bearish signal. Post-bubble damage control emphasized the critical nature of using technical indicators, like the Relative Strength Index (RSI) and MACD, to navigate speculative bubbles and identify exit points.

The 2008 Financial Crisis

The financial crisis of 2008 was triggered by the bursting of the housing bubble and the collapse of Lehman Brothers. This event led to a severe global economic downturn. The S&P 500 lost nearly 57% from its 2007 peak to its 2009 trough, erasing trillions of dollars in market capitalization.

The crisis reshaped the landscape of risk management and fundamentally altered market psychology. Technical analysts observed the early signs, such as the breakdown of key support levels and the head-and-shoulders patterns that flagged impending trouble. Understanding these technical signals emphasized the importance of exit strategies and diversification to mitigate systemic risk.

The Rise of Bitcoin

Bitcoin, the first cryptocurrency, emerged from the 2008 financial crisis as a decentralized alternative to traditional financial systems. Rapid adoption and speculative interest led to a parabolic rise, with Bitcoin reaching an all-time high near $20,000 in December 2017 before plummeting thereafter.

Bitcoin's volatile history provided a fertile ground for technical analysis. Traders employed trendlines, moving averages, and Fibonacci retracements extensively to navigate Bitcoin's boom and bust cycles. The asset's high volatility highlighted the effectiveness of tools like the Average True Range (ATR) for setting stop-loss levels and managing risk in highly speculative markets.

COVID-19 Market Reaction

The COVID-19 pandemic in 2020 caused one of the most rapid market declines in history, followed by an equally swift recovery. The S&P 500 fell approximately 34% in just over a month but then rallied to new highs within the same year, driven by unprecedented monetary and fiscal stimulus.

This period underscored the importance of combining technical analysis with macroeconomic understanding. Traders who recognized the formation of V-shaped recoveries and double-bottom patterns could capitalize on the rapid shifts. Moreover, the crisis emphasized the value of diversification and maintaining a flexible trading strategy adaptable to fast-changing conditions.

In sum, these case studies provide rich lessons in the dynamics of market behavior. They're not just historical footnotes but essential guides for developing technical acumen, sharpening risk management skills, and shaping a resilient trading mindset. By studying these events, traders and investors are better equipped to navigate future market challenges with confidence and insight.

www.ingramcontent.com/pod-product-compliance
Lightning Source LLC
Chambersburg PA
CBHW030529210326
41597CB00013B/1084